The Usborne
Children's book of Baking

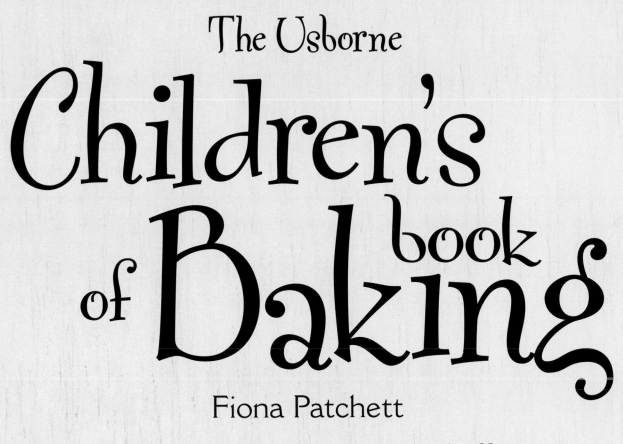

Fiona Patchett

Designed by Nancy Leschnikoff

Photography by Howard Allman
Illustrated by Molly Sage and Adam Larkum

Recipes and food preparation by Catherine Atkinson

Contents

Biscuits and other treats

Cakes

Decorating tips

Pastry and tarts

Bread and buns

Getting started

The mouth-watering recipes in this book are ideal for anyone new to baking. Each recipe is explained simply, without using baffling cooking terms. Throughout the book, chefs offer you handy hints, and you can find explanations of some useful baking skills on pages 94-95. Read these pages first, then get baking!

Always wash fruit before you use it in a recipe.

Weighing and measuring

Before you start, read through the recipe and check that you've got all the ingredients listed at the beginning, as well as the equipment you will need. If a recipe lists softened butter, take it out of the fridge 30 minutes before you use it. That will make it easier to stir into the other ingredients.

When you are baking, it is important that you measure things out exactly and don't leave anything out – otherwise your cakes and biscuits might not turn out quite right. Weigh dry ingredients on kitchen scales and measure liquids in a measuring jug.

Keeping clean

Try to keep everything clean when you are baking. Put things away after you have used them. If you spill anything, wipe it up straight away. And always wash your hands before you start.

Measuring spoons are the easiest way to measure out spoonfuls.

The ingredient should lie level with the top of the spoon.

Preparing tins and trays

If you are making a cake, use the size and shape of tin suggested in the recipe. If you use a different size, you may not have enough mixture. Most of the recipes involve greasing and lining the tin. This stops the food from sticking to the tin. You grease and line baking trays in the same way.

1. To grease a cake tin, dip a paper towel into soft butter or cooking oil. Rub the towel over the insides of the tin.

Cut just inside the pencil line.

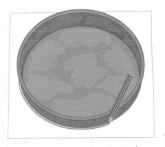

2. To line the tin, put it onto a sheet of baking parchment. Draw around it with a pencil. Cut out the shape and lay it inside the tin.

Cooking times

If you have a fan oven, you may need to lower the temperature or shorten the cooking time. Look in the instruction book to see what is recommended. Do not open the oven door, unless the recipe tells you, or you think something might be burning.

Which shelf?

Always use the middle shelf of an oven, unless the recipe says something else. If you need to use two shelves, cook the food on the middle shelf for the time the recipe says, then take it out. Move the food on the bottom shelf up until it is cooked.

Storing

When your cakes, pastries, biscuits or bread have cooled, you can store them in an airtight container or put them in the freezer. Anything you make that contains fresh cream should be served immediately, or kept in the fridge.

Gingerbread flowers

You can make these gingerbread flowers look really pretty by decorating them with different coloured icing. If you like really gingery cookies, add extra ginger instead of cinnamon.

Ingredients:

Makes 25 biscuits

350g (12oz) plain flour
1½ teaspoons ground ginger
½ teaspoon ground cinnamon
1 teaspoon bicarbonate of soda
100g (4oz) chilled butter or
    margarine
175g (6oz) light muscovado sugar
1 medium egg
2 tablespoons golden syrup
writing icing

a flower-shaped cookie cutter

Chef's Tip

Use a kitchen towel to wipe a little cooking oil over a measuring spoon before you measure the syrup. It will help the syrup slide off the spoon more easily.

1. Heat the oven to 180°C, 350°F, gas mark 4. Use a paper towel to wipe a little oil over two baking trays. Use a sieve to sift the flour into a large mixing bowl.

2. Sift the ginger, cinnamon and bicarbonate of soda into the bowl too. Cut the butter or margarine into chunks and stir it in so that it is coated with flour.

3. Use your fingertips to rub the chunks of butter or margarine into the flour, until the mixture looks like fine breadcrumbs. Then, stir in the sugar.

4. Break the egg into a small bowl and beat it with a fork. Add the syrup to the egg and beat it in. Add the eggy mixture to the flour, then mix everything together.

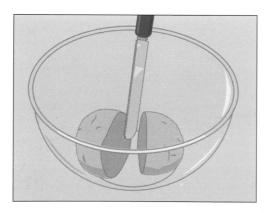

5. Holding the bowl in one hand, use your other hand to squeeze the mixture together until you have a smooth dough. Use a blunt knife to cut the dough in half.

6. Sprinkle a little flour onto a clean work surface and put one piece of the dough onto it. Then, roll out the dough until it is about 5mm (¼in) thick.

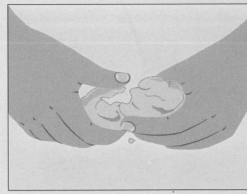

7. Use a flower-shaped cookie cutter to cut out lots of flower shapes from the dough. Use a spatula to lift the shapes onto the baking trays.

8. Roll out the other half of the dough and cut more flower shapes from it. Squeeze the scraps of dough together to make a ball. Roll it out and cut more shapes.

9. Put the biscuits into your oven and bake them for 12-15 minutes, until they are dark golden. Leave the biscuits on the trays for five minutes to cool.

10. Use a spatula to lift the biscuits onto a wire rack. When they are cold, draw patterns on them with writing icing, or make your own icing to pipe on (see page 72).

Orange shortbread stars

To make these traditional Scottish biscuits, you will need to rub the butter into the flour with your fingertips. This recipe makes biscuits with a zesty orange flavour, but you could try it with lemon or lime.

Ingredients:

Makes 14 biscuits

150g (5oz) plain flour
25g (1oz) semolina or
   ground rice
100g (4oz) chilled butter
1 small orange
50g (2oz) caster sugar

a 7½cm (3in) star-shaped
   cutter

1. Heat the oven to 170°C, 325°F, gas mark 3. Use a paper towel to wipe a little oil over two baking trays. Sift the flour through a sieve into a large bowl.

2. Sift the semolina or ground rice into the bowl too. Cut the butter into chunks and put it into the bowl. Use a wooden spoon to coat the butter with flour.

3. Rub the butter between your fingertips. Lift the mixture and let it fall back into the bowl as you rub. Carry on until the mixture looks like fine breadcrumbs.

4. Use the medium-sized holes of a grater to grate the rind of the orange onto a small plate. Add the rind and the sugar to the mixture in the large bowl.

5. Cut the orange in half and squeeze the juice from one half. Sprinkle two teaspoons of the juice over the other ingredients, then stir everything together.

6. Holding the bowl in one hand, use your other hand to squeeze the dough into a ball. The heat from your hand makes the dough stick together.

7. Sprinkle some flour onto a clean work surface and onto a rolling pin. Put the dough onto the work surface and roll it out until it is 5mm (¼in) thick.

Chef's Tip

8. Use a star-shaped cutter to cut out lots of star shapes from the dough. Lift them onto a baking tray with a spatula. Then, squeeze the scraps into a ball.

If you want to make dots around the edge of your biscuits, use a toothpick or fork to press holes. This also helps stop little bubbles appearing on the surface.

9. Roll out the dough and cut out more stars. Bake the biscuits for 12-15 minutes. Leave them for two minutes, then lift them onto a wire rack to cool.

Chocolate and cherry cookies

These cookies are very easy to make. They are sometimes known as drop cookies because the dough can be dropped with a spoon onto the baking trays.

Rich chocolate and tangy cherries taste delicious together, but you could try other combinations, such as white chocolate and dried cranberries, or hazelnut pieces and chopped apricots.

Ingredients:

Makes 24 cookies

75g (3oz) butter, softened
75g (3oz) caster sugar
75g (3oz) soft light brown sugar
1 medium egg
1 teaspoon vanilla essence
175g (6oz) plain flour
½ teaspoon baking powder
50g (2oz) dried cherries
100g (4oz) milk or plain
　chocolate drops

1. Heat the oven to 180°C, 350°F, gas mark 4. Use a paper towel to wipe a little oil over two baking trays. Put the butter and both types of sugar into a large mixing bowl.

2. Stir the butter and sugar together with a wooden spoon until the mixture is smooth and creamy. Break the egg into a small bowl and beat it well with a fork.

3. Add the vanilla essence to the egg and mix it in. Then, add the eggy mixture to the large bowl, a little at a time, stirring it well between each addition.

4. Sift the flour and baking powder through a sieve into the bowl. Stir the mixture until it is smooth. Cut the cherries in half and add them to the mixture too.

Chef's Tip

You can make the cherries softer and less chewy by soaking them in orange juice. Soak them for about an hour, then use a small sieve to drain off the juice.

Make sure the cookies are well spaced out on the baking trays.

5. Add 50g (2oz) of the chocolate drops to the mixture and stir them in well. Then, put a heaped teaspoon of the mixture onto one of the baking trays.

6. Use the rest of the mixture to make more cookies. Flatten each cookie with the back of a fork and sprinkle them with the remaining chocolate drops.

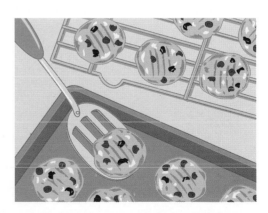

7. Bake the cookies in the oven for 10 minutes until they are golden brown. Leave them on the trays for a few minutes. Use a spatula to lift them onto a wire rack to cool.

Lace biscuits with lime cream

These biscuits spread out as they cook to make a pretty, lacy pattern. They have an oaty, buttery taste. You can serve them as they are, or sandwich them with lime cream, made from mascarpone.

Ingredients:

Makes 16 biscuits

For the biscuits:
75g (3oz) butter
75g (3oz) porridge oats
100g (4oz) caster sugar
1 medium egg
2 teaspoons plain flour
1 teaspoon baking powder

For the lime cream:
1 lime
250g (9oz) mascarpone
25g (1oz) icing sugar

You could make the filling with orange or lemon instead of lime.

Cut out the rectangles just inside your pencil lines.

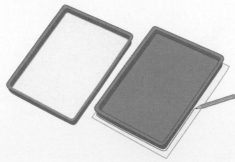

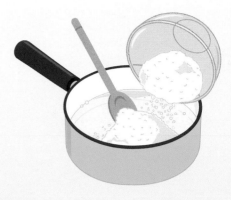

1. Heat the oven to 170°C, 325°F, gas mark 3. Put two baking trays on baking parchment. Draw around them. Cut out the shapes and lay them in the baking trays.

2. Put the butter into a saucepan. Place it over a low heat until the butter has melted. Take the pan off the heat. Then, stir in the oats with a wooden spoon.

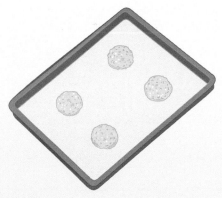

3. Add the sugar to the pan and stir it in. Leave the mixture to stand for two or three minutes. This gives the butter enough time to soak into the oats.

4. Break the egg into a small bowl and beat it with a fork. Stir the beaten egg into the oaty mixture. Sift in the flour and baking powder over the mixture and stir them in.

5. Put four heaped teaspoons of the mixture onto each baking tray, making sure they are well spaced out. Bake them for 9-10 minutes until they are a deep golden brown.

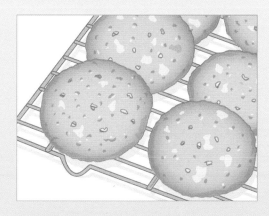

6. Leave the biscuits to cool on the baking trays for five minutes. Then, carefully lift them off the paper using a blunt knife. Put them onto a wire rack to cool.

7. Leave the baking parchment on the baking trays. Follow steps 5 and 6 to bake more biscuits. Leave all the biscuits on the wire rack to cool completely.

8. While the biscuits are cooling, make the filling, following the recipe on page 74. Spread some of the lime cream onto the flat side of one biscuit.

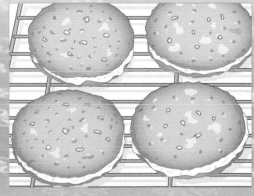

9. Put another biscuit on top of the filling to sandwich the biscuits together. Sandwich together all the biscuits. Serve them before the filling makes the biscuits soggy.

Viennese biscuits

These biscuits have a smooth filling, known as ganache – a French word for a mixture of chocolate and cream.

Ingredients:

Makes 24 biscuits (12 pairs)

For the biscuits:
175g (6oz) unsalted
 butter, softened
40g (1½oz) icing sugar
1 teaspoon vanilla essence
175g (6oz) plain flour
40g (1½oz) cornflour

For the ganache:
75g (3oz) plain or milk
 chocolate drops
4 tablespoons double cream

  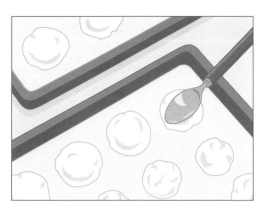

1. Heat the oven to 190°C, 375°F, gas mark 5. Grease and line two baking trays. Put the butter in a bowl. Sift the icing sugar over it. Beat the mixture until it is creamy.

2. Stir in the vanilla essence. Sift the flour and cornflour over the mixture. Stir them in until they are smooth. Put a teaspoon of the mixture onto one of the trays.

3. Put more teaspoons of mixture onto the trays, leaving spaces between them. Flatten each blob of mixture slightly with the back of a teaspoon.

4. Bake the biscuits for 12-14 minutes, until they are pale golden brown. Leave them on their trays for five minutes, then use a spatula to lift them onto a wire rack.

5. For the ganache, put the chocolate drops in a heatproof bowl and add the cream. Then, pour about 5cm (2in) water into a saucepan.

6. Heat the water until it bubbles, then take the pan off the heat. Carefully, put the bowl inside the pan. Stir the chocolate and cream until the chocolate has melted.

 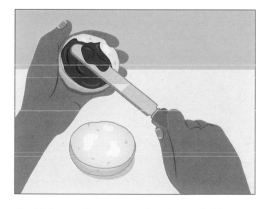 

7. Lift the bowl out of the pan and let the ganache cool for a few minutes. Then, put it in the fridge for about an hour, stirring it every now and then, as it thickens.

8. When the ganache is soft like butter, take it out of the fridge. Use a blunt knife to spread some onto the flat side of a biscuit. Press another biscuit on top.

9. Sandwich the biscuits together in pairs until all the ganache and biscuits are used up. Eat them straight away, or keep them in an airtight container in the fridge.

Jammy cut-out biscuits

These biscuits have cut-out shapes on top, so you can see the jammy filling. You could try this recipe with different kinds of jam and any shape of cutter you like.

Ingredients:

Makes about 10 biscuits

100g (4oz) butter, softened
50g (2oz) caster sugar
1 orange
1 medium egg
2 tablespoons ground almonds
   (optional)
200g (7oz) plain flour
1 tablespoon of cornflour
8 tablespoons seedless
   raspberry jam

a 5cm (2in) round cutter
small shaped cutters

1. Heat the oven to 180°C, 350°F, gas mark 4. Grease two baking trays. Put the butter and sugar into a large bowl. Mix them until the mixture is creamy.

2. Grate the rind of the orange using the medium holes of a grater, trying not to grate the white part underneath. Add the rind to the bowl and stir it in.

3. Break the egg into a cup. Mix the yolk and white with a fork, then add a little to the mixture in the bowl. Mix it in well, then add some more and mix that in.

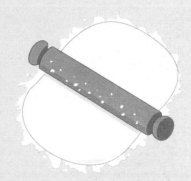

4. Carry on until you have added all the egg. Add the ground almonds to the bowl, if you are using them. Use a sieve to sift the flour and cornflour on top.

5. Mix everything together with your hands, until you have made a dough. Wrap the dough in plastic foodwrap and put it in a fridge to chill for 30 minutes.

6. Sprinkle some flour onto a clean work surface and rolling pin. Then, use the rolling pin to roll out the dough until it is about 3mm (1/8in) thick.

7. Using the round cutter, cut out lots of circles. Then, use the shaped cutters to cut holes in the middle of half the circles. Squeeze the scraps into a ball.

8. Roll out the ball and cut more circles. Put all the circles on the baking trays. Bake the biscuits for 15 minutes. Leave them on the baking trays for two minutes.

9. Lift the biscuits onto a wire rack to cool. Then, spread jam on the whole biscuits, as far as the edge. Place a cut-out biscuit on each one and press it down gently.

Lemon spiral biscuits

To make these pretty, lemony biscuits, you roll together a layer of pink dough and a layer of white dough. Then, you cut the roll into slices to make biscuits with a spiral pattern.

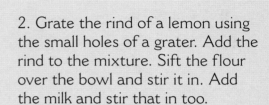

Ingredients:

Makes 40 biscuits

75g (3oz) icing sugar
150g (5oz) butter, softened
1 lemon
200g (7oz) plain flour
2 tablespoons milk
pink food dye

1. Grease two baking trays. Using a sieve, sift the icing sugar into a large mixing bowl. Add the butter and mix it in until the mixture is smooth and creamy.

2. Grate the rind of a lemon using the small holes of a grater. Add the rind to the mixture. Sift the flour over the bowl and stir it in. Add the milk and stir that in too.

3. Put half the mixture into another bowl. Add three drops of pink food dye to one of the bowls. Stir it in until the mixture is completely pink.

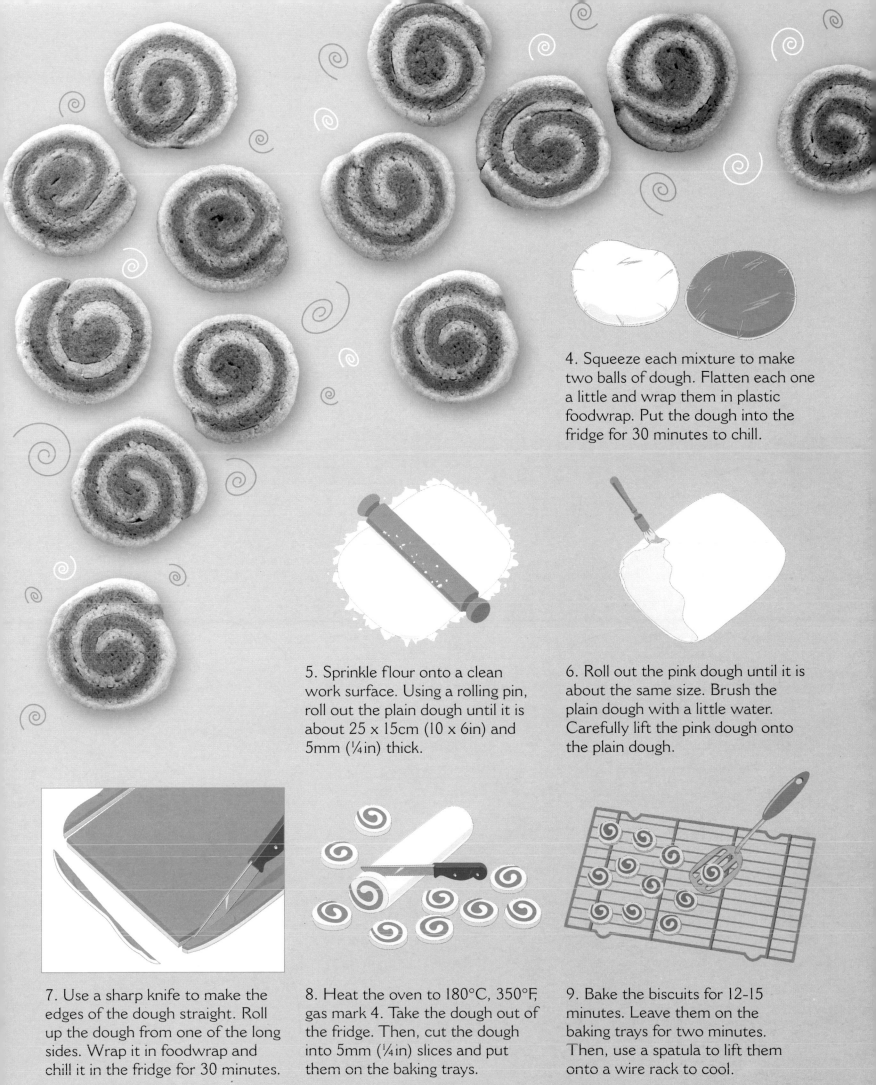

4. Squeeze each mixture to make two balls of dough. Flatten each one a little and wrap them in plastic foodwrap. Put the dough into the fridge for 30 minutes to chill.

5. Sprinkle flour onto a clean work surface. Using a rolling pin, roll out the plain dough until it is about 25 x 15cm (10 x 6in) and 5mm (¼in) thick.

6. Roll out the pink dough until it is about the same size. Brush the plain dough with a little water. Carefully lift the pink dough onto the plain dough.

7. Use a sharp knife to make the edges of the dough straight. Roll up the dough from one of the long sides. Wrap it in foodwrap and chill it in the fridge for 30 minutes.

8. Heat the oven to 180°C, 350°F, gas mark 4. Take the dough out of the fridge. Then, cut the dough into 5mm (¼in) slices and put them on the baking trays.

9. Bake the biscuits for 12-15 minutes. Leave them on the baking trays for two minutes. Then, use a spatula to lift them onto a wire rack to cool.

Macaroon creams

These macaroons are filled with pale shades of buttercream and will just melt in your mouth.

Ingredients:

Makes 36 biscuits (18 pairs)

For the macaroons:
2 medium-sized eggs
175g (6oz) caster sugar
125g (4½oz) ground almonds
25g (1oz) ground rice

For the buttercream:
50g (2oz) butter, softened
100g (4oz) icing sugar
pink, yellow and green food dye

1. Heat the oven to 150°C, 300°F, gas mark 2. Put two baking trays on baking parchment. Use a pencil to draw around them. Cut out the shapes and lay them in the trays.

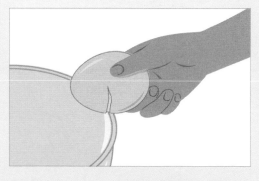

2. To separate the first egg white from the yolk, break the egg on the edge of a bowl. Slide the egg slowly onto a small plate. Then, put an egg cup over the yolk.

You don't need to
keep the yolks.

3. Holding the egg cup, tip the plate over the bowl, so that the egg white dribbles into it. Do the same with the other egg, so that both the whites are in the bowl.

4. Whisk the egg whites with a whisk until they are really thick. When you lift the whisk up, the egg whites should make stiff peaks, like this.

5. Add the caster sugar, ground almonds and ground rice to the egg whites. Then, use a metal spoon to fold the ingredients together gently.

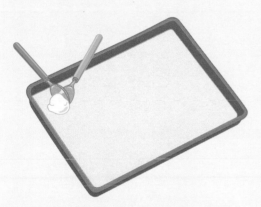

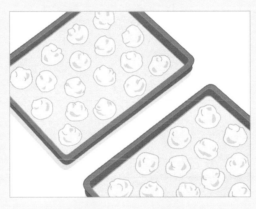

6. Scoop up a slightly rounded teaspoon of the mixture. Using another teaspoon, push the mixture off the spoon and onto one of the baking trays.

7. Make more macaroons in the same way, making sure they are well spaced out on the trays. Put them in the oven and bake them for 20 minutes.

8. When the macaroons are pale golden in colour, take them out of the oven. Leave them on the trays for five minutes. Then, lift them onto a wire rack to cool.

Use a wooden spoon to
beat the mixture.

Use a blunt knife to spread the buttercream.

9. For the buttercream, put the butter in a bowl. Beat it until it is creamy. Sift the icing sugar into the bowl, then beat the mixture until it is fluffy.

10. Divide the mixture between three bowls. Add two drops of pink food dye to one bowl, two drops of yellow to another and two drops of green to another. Mix it all in.

11. Spread some buttercream on the flat side of a macaroon. Then, press another macaroon on top. Sandwich all the macaroons with different colours of buttercream.

Crunchy peanut cookies

These sweet and nutty cookies get their crunchy texture from peanut butter and puffed rice cereal. Make them with unsalted butter, as peanut butter contains quite a lot of salt already.

Ingredients:

Makes 20 cookies

1 medium egg
100g (4oz) unsalted butter
100g (4oz) soft light brown sugar
100g (4oz) crunchy peanut butter
150g (5oz) self-raising flour
½ teaspoon baking powder
50g (2oz) puffed rice cereal

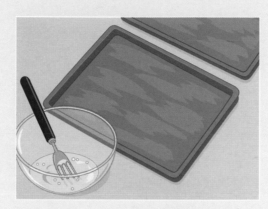

1. Heat the oven to 190°C, 375°F, gas mark 5. Use a paper towel to wipe a little oil over two baking trays. Break the egg into a small bowl and beat it well with a fork.

Use a wooden spoon to beat the mixture.

2. Put the butter and sugar into a bowl. Beat them until they are creamy. Add the egg a little at a time. Beat it after each addition to stop the mixture getting lumpy.

3. Add the peanut butter to the mixture and beat it until it is well mixed in. Then, sift the flour and baking powder over the mixture. Stir everything together.

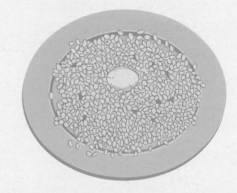

4. Put the puffed rice cereal onto a plate. Scoop up a heaped teaspoon of the mixture and shape it into a ball with your hands. Put it on top of the cereal.

Leave plenty of space between the balls of mixture.

5. Roll the mixture in the cereal to cover it. Flatten it very slightly and place it on one of the baking trays. Make more balls and place them on the baking trays.

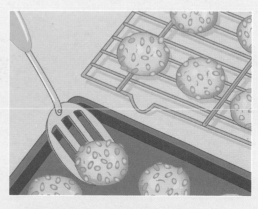

6. Bake the cookies for 20 minutes. Leave them on the baking trays for five minutes. Then, use a spatula to lift them onto a wire rack to cool.

These crunchy peanut
cookies are delicious
served with hot
chocolate.

23

Chocolate marzipan hearts

These may look like ordinary chocolate biscuits, but when you bite into them, you'll discover a delicious marzipan middle.

1. Use a paper towel to wipe oil over a baking tray. Sift the flour and cocoa powder into a large bowl. Cut the butter into chunks and add them to the mixture.

2. Stir the butter into the mixture, so it is coated with flour. Rub the butter with your fingertips until the mixture looks like fine breadcrumbs. Stir in the sugar.

Ingredients:

Makes 20 hearts

100g (4oz) self-raising flour
25g (1oz) cocoa powder
75g (3oz) chilled butter
50g (2oz) caster sugar
1 medium egg
100g (4oz) marzipan
1 teaspoon icing sugar
½ teaspoon cocoa powder

a medium and a small
   heart-shaped cutter

You do not need the egg white in this recipe.

3. Break the egg onto a plate. Hold an egg cup over the yolk and tip the plate over a small bowl, so the egg white slides off. Add the yolk to the mixture.

4. Stir the mixture into a dough. Then, use your hands to squeeze the dough into a ball. Wrap it in plastic foodwrap and put it in the fridge to chill for 30 minutes.

Chef's Tip

Instead of throwing away an egg white, you can use it in other recipes, such as swirly meringues on page 32 or macaroon creams on page 20.

5. Sprinkle some icing sugar onto a clean work surface and a rolling pin. Roll out the marzipan until it is 3mm (1/8in) thick. Cut out some hearts with the smaller cutter.

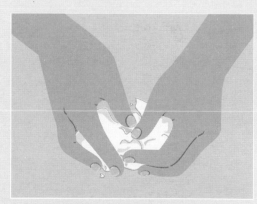

6. Squeeze the scraps of marzipan together into a ball. Roll it out again and cut out more hearts. You will need 12. Then, heat the oven to 200°C, 400°F, gas mark 6.

You may need to press hard to squash the dough together.

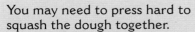

7. Sprinkle some flour onto a clean work surface and a rolling pin. Roll out the dough until it is 3mm (1/8in) thick. Use the larger cutter to cut out 24 hearts.

8. Put half the chocolate hearts on the baking tray. Put a marzipan heart on each one. Put a second chocolate heart on top. Press the edges of each biscuit together.

9. Bake the biscuits for ten minutes. When they are ready, sift a little icing sugar over them, then sift a little cocoa powder over that. Lift them onto a wire rack to cool.

Iced lemon biscuits

These biscuits have a crisp, yet buttery texture. You could cover them with lemon icing and decorate them with yellow and white writing icing and sweets.

Ingredients:

Makes 30 biscuits

For the biscuits:
1 medium lemon
125g (4½oz) plain flour
50g (2oz) icing sugar
1 medium egg
100g (4oz) butter, softened

For the lemon icing:
200g (7oz) icing sugar
3 tablespoons lemon juice
yellow food dye
white and yellow writing icing
white and yellow sweets

a 4cm (1½in) round cutter

1. Wipe a little oil over two baking trays with a paper towel. Grate the rind of the lemon onto a small plate, using the medium-sized holes of a grater.

2. Sift the flour and icing sugar into a large mixing bowl and stir in the lemon rind. Cut the lemon in half and squeeze the juice into a small bowl.

You do not need the egg white in this recipe.

3. Break the egg onto a plate. Hold an egg cup over the yolk and tip the saucer over a bowl, so the egg white slides off. Add the yolk to the mixture in the large bowl.

4. Add the butter and a tablespoon of lemon juice. Stir the mixture with a wooden spoon until it is smooth. Scoop the mixture into a ball with your hands and flatten it slightly.

5. Wrap the dough in plastic foodwrap and put it in the fridge to chill for 30 minutes. While the dough is chilling, heat the oven to 190°C, 375°F, gas mark 5.

6. Dust a clean work surface and a rolling pin with flour. Take the dough out of the fridge. Use the rolling pin to roll out the dough until it is 5mm (¼in) thick.

7. Use the cutter to cut out lots of circles, then use a blunt knife to lift the circles onto the baking trays. Squeeze the scraps of dough into a ball and roll it out again.

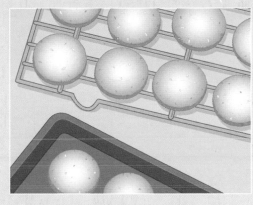

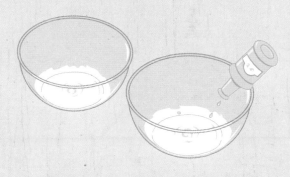

8. Cut out more circles and put them on the trays. Bake the biscuits in the oven for 8-10 minutes until they are golden. Then, take them out of the oven.

9. Leave the biscuits on the baking trays for five minutes. Use a spatula to lift them onto a wire rack. To make the lemon icing, sift the icing sugar into a small bowl.

10. Stir three tablespoons of lemon juice into the icing sugar. Put half the mixture into another bowl. Add two drops of yellow food dye to one bowl and mix it in.

11. Use a teaspoon to spread a little icing on top of one biscuit. Ice half the biscuits with white icing and half with yellow icing. Leave the icing to dry.

12. Decorate the biscuits with white and yellow writing icing and sweets. You can find out how to pipe icing patterns onto biscuits on page 72.

Chocolate florentines

These biscuits can be varied by using different fruits and nuts. You could use different coloured glacé cherries or tropical glacé fruits, but keep the total weight of the fruit and nuts the same.

Ingredients:

Makes 12 florentines

8 glacé cherries
25g (1oz) butter
25g (1oz) demerara sugar
25g (1oz) golden syrup
25g (1oz) plain flour
40g (1½oz) mixed candied peel
40g (1½oz) flaked almonds
75g (3oz) plain chocolate drops

1. Heat the oven to 180°C, 350°F, gas mark 4. Grease two baking trays. Cover them with parchment. Put the cherries onto a chopping board. Cut them into quarters.

2. Put the butter, sugar and syrup into a pan. Gently heat the ingredients until everything has just melted. Then, remove the pan from the heat.

Make sure the biscuits are well-spaced out.

3. Add the flour, cherries, candied peel and almonds to the pan. Stir everything together. Spoon teaspoonfuls of the mixture onto the baking trays.

4. Bake the florentines for ten minutes until they are a deep golden colour. Use a blunt knife to push in any wavy edges. Leave them to cool for two minutes.

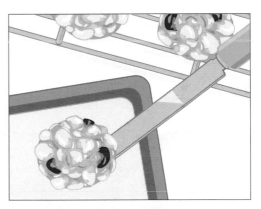

5. Lift the florentines onto a cooling rack. Then, pour about 5cm (2in) of water into a pan. Heat the pan until the water bubbles. Remove the pan from the heat.

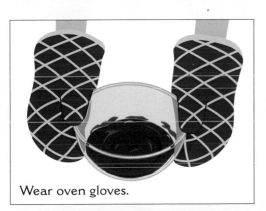

Wear oven gloves.

6. Put the chocolate drops into a heatproof bowl. Carefully put the bowl inside the pan. Stir the chocolate until it has melted. Take the bowl out of the pan.

7. Use a teaspoon to spread melted chocolate over the flat base of each florentine. Then, use a fork to make zig-zag patterns in the chocolate.

8. Place the florentines on a sheet of baking parchment, making sure the chocolate side is facing upwards. Wait until the chocolate dries before you serve them.

Apple flapjack

These fruity flapjacks contain fresh apple, sultanas and cinnamon. To make flapjacks, you melt some of the ingredients together in a pan, before putting them in the oven.

Ingredients:

Makes 12 flapjacks

2 eating apples
175g (6oz) butter
175g (6oz) demerara sugar
2 tablespoons golden syrup
½ teaspoon ground cinnamon
50g (2oz) sultanas
225g (8oz) porridge oats
2 tablespoons sunflower seeds
  (optional)

an 18 x 27cm (7 x 11in) tin

Chef's Tip

Flapjacks should be dark golden brown and soft when you take them out of the oven. If you cook them too long, they may be dry and not so chewy.

1. Heat the oven to 160°C, 325°F, gas mark 3. Put the tin on some baking parchment and use a pencil to draw around it. Cut out the rectangle of parchment.

Use a wooden spoon to stir the mixture.

3. Put the chunks of apple in a saucepan with 25g (1oz) of the butter. Cook them over a low heat for ten minutes, stirring every now and then, until the apple is soft.

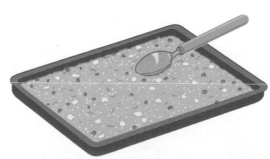

5. Stir in the oats. Add the seeds, if you are using them. Stir everything together. Spoon the mixture into the tin and spread it out. Smooth the top with the back of a spoon.

2. Grease the tin and lay the parchment inside. Cut the apple into quarters. Peel them, then cut out the cores. Cut the quarters into small chunks.

4. Add the rest of the butter with the sugar, syrup, cinnamon and sultanas. Heat the mixture gently until the butter has melted. Then, take the pan off the heat.

6. Put the tin on the middle shelf of the oven and bake it for 25 minutes. Take it out of the oven, leave it for ten minutes to cool. Then, cut the mixture into pieces.

Swirly meringues

These meringues are crispy on the outside, but soft and chewy on the inside. They have chocolate swirled through them to make them look marbled.

Ingredients:

Makes 12 meringues

50g (2oz) plain chocolate drops
2 medium eggs
100g (4oz) caster sugar

Cut out the shape just inside your pencil line.

1. Heat the oven to 110°C, 225°F, gas mark ½. Lay two baking trays on baking parchment. Draw around them. Cut out the shapes and lay them on the baking trays.

2. Pour about 5cm (2in) water into a saucepan. Heat the water until it bubbles, then take the pan off the heat. Put the chocolate drops into a heatproof bowl.

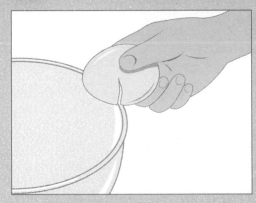

You don't use the yolks in this recipe.

Use a wooden spoon to stir the chocolate.

3. Carefully, put the bowl inside the pan. Stir the chocolate until it has melted. Then, take the bowl out of the pan and leave it to cool while you make the meringues.

4. To separate the egg white from the yolk, break one egg on the edge of a bowl. Slide the egg slowly onto a small plate. Then, put an egg cup over the yolk.

5. Hold the egg cup and tip the plate over the bowl, so that the egg white dribbles into it. Do the same with the other egg, so that both the whites are in the bowl.

6. Whisk the egg whites with a whisk until they are really thick. When you lift the whisk up, the egg whites should make stiff peaks, like this.

7. Add a heaped teaspoon of sugar to the egg whites. Whisk it in well. Keep adding spoonfuls of sugar and whisking them in, until you have added all the sugar.

8. Drizzle teaspoons of the melted chocolate over the top of the meringue mixture. Stir the mixture once or twice to marble it with the chocolate.

Leave the merinuges on the trays to cool.

Chef's Tip

9. Scoop up a spoonful of the meringue mixture with a dessertspoon. Then, using a teaspoon, push the mixture off onto one of the baking trays.

10. Make eleven more meringues and put them in the oven to bake for 40 minutes. Turn off the oven and leave them inside. After 15 minutes, take them out to cool.

When you whisk egg whites, try adding a 'pinch' of salt – the amount you can pick up between your first finger and thumb – to help them stiffen.

Victoria sponge cake

This classic sponge cake is named after Queen Victoria. To make it, you start by beating the butter and sugar together until they are light and fluffy. This traps lots of little air bubbles in the mixture, which helps the cake to rise.

Ingredients:

Makes 10 slices

For the sponge:
4 medium eggs
225g (8oz) butter, softened
225g (8oz) caster sugar
225g (8oz) self-raising flour

For the filling:
100g (4oz) unsalted butter, softened
225g (8oz) icing sugar
1 tablespoon milk
½ teaspoon vanilla essence
4 tablespoons raspberry or strawberry jam

extra caster sugar, for sprinkling over the cake

two 20cm (8in) round, shallow cake tins

1. Heat the oven to 180°C, 350°F, gas mark 4. Wipe the insides of the tins with cooking oil. Put one tin onto some baking parchment and draw around it with a pencil.

2. Cut out the circle, then do the same again. Put one paper circle in each tin. Break the eggs into a small bowl. Beat them together with a fork.

Chef's Tip

In the next step, you'll add the eggs to a mixture. Add them slowly to stop the mixture from getting lumpy. If it does get lumpy, stir in a teaspoonful of flour.

3. Put the butter and sugar in a large mixing bowl and beat them until they are pale and fluffy. Add the eggs a little at a time, beating well after each addition.

4. Sift the flour over the mixture. Gently fold it in with a metal spoon. Then, divide the mixture equally between the tins. Smooth the tops with the back of a spoon.

If the cakes are cooked, they will spring back when pressed.

5. Bake the cakes in the oven for 25 minutes. Wearing oven gloves, carefully take the cakes out of the oven. Press the cakes with a finger to see if they are cooked.

34

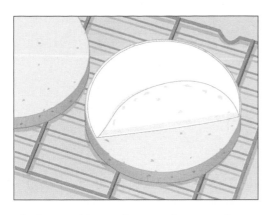

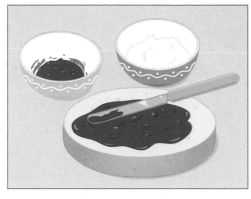

6. Leave the cakes in the tins for five minutes to cool. Then, run a knife around the edges and turn them out onto a wire rack. Peel off the baking parchment.

7. Put the jam in a bowl and beat it. Spread it over one cake. Make the vanilla buttercream (see page 75), then spread it over the flat side of the other cake.

8. Sandwich both cakes together, with the jam and buttercream inside. Gently press the cakes together. Use a teapsoon to scatter caster sugar over the top.

Fairy cakes

These pretty cakes are really easy to make because all the ingredients are simply beaten together. You can ice them with different colours of icing and decorate them with sugar flowers, fresh fruit and piped icing.

Ingredients:

Makes 12 cakes

90g (3½oz) self-raising flour
90g (3½oz) caster sugar
90g (3½oz) soft margarine
2 medium eggs
½ teaspoon vanilla essence

For the icing:
175g (6oz) icing sugar
1½ tablespoons warm water
yellow food dye
small sugar flowers

a 12-hole shallow bun tray
paper cake cases

1. Heat the oven to 190°C, 375°F, gas mark 5. Put a paper case into each hole in the tray. Use a sieve to sift the flour into a large bowl. Add the sugar, margarine and vanilla.

2. Break the eggs into a cup, then add them to the bowl. Stir everything together with a wooden spoon until the mixture is smooth and creamy.

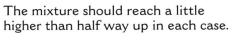

The mixture should reach a little higher than half way up in each case.

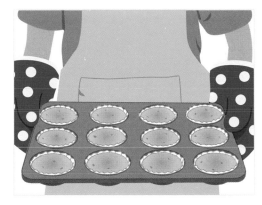

3. Use a teaspoon to divide the mixture between the paper cake cases. Bake the cakes in the oven for 15 minutes, until they are firm and golden.

4. Wearing oven gloves, carefully take the cakes out of the oven. Leave them in the tray for a few minutes. Then, lift them out of the tray onto a wire rack to cool.

5. To make white icing, sift the icing sugar into a bowl. Stir in the warm water to make a smooth, white paste. Use a teaspoon to ice four of the cakes.

Chef's Tip

6. To make pale yellow icing, add two drops of yellow food dye to the bowl and stir it in well. Use a teaspoon to ice four more cakes with pale yellow icing.

7. To make darker yellow icing, add two more drops of yellow dye and stir it in well. Spread it onto the last four cakes. Then decorate all the cakes.

To give the icing a smooth surface, dip a blunt knife into warm water and slide it over the cakes. You can dip the teaspoon in water too, to stop it from getting sticky.

Lemon and lime cupcakes

These little cakes are drizzled with lemon and lime syrup, then covered with a luscious layer of icing.

Ingredients:

Makes 12 cupcakes

For the cakes:
90g (4oz) self-raising flour
90g (4oz) caster sugar
90g (4oz) soft margarine
1 tablespoon milk
2 medium eggs

For the lemon and lime syrup:
1 lemon
1 lime
25g (1oz) caster sugar

For the lemon and lime icing:
175g (6oz) icing sugar
15g (½oz) butter

a 12-hole shallow bun tray
paper cake cases

Chef's Tip

To make a large drizzle cake, make the Victoria sponge on pages 34-35. Then, follow steps 4-8 on these pages to add the lemon and lime syrup.

1. Heat the oven to 190°C, 375°F, gas mark 5. Put a paper case into each hole in the baking tray. Use a sieve to sift the flour into a large mixing bowl.

Use a wooden spoon to stir the mixture.

2. Add the sugar, margarine and milk to the large bowl. Break the eggs into a cup. Add them to the bowl too. Stir the mixture until it is light and fluffy.

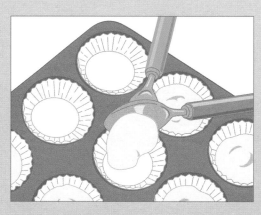

3. Use a teaspoon to divide the mixture between the paper cases. Bake the cakes in the oven for about 12 minutes. When they are golden, take them out of the oven.

A zester gives you long pieces of rind.

4. After a few minutes, lift the cakes onto a wire rack. To make the syrup, grate the rind of the lemon and lime, or scrape some off with a zester, if you have one.

5. Put two-thirds of the lemon and lime rind onto a small plate. Cover it with plastic foodwrap and put it to one side to use later. Put the rest of the rind in a small pan.

6. Cut the lemon and lime in half. Squeeze the juice from them. Add the sugar and three tablespoons of the juice to the pan. Heat it gently until the sugar has dissolved.

7. Remove the pan from the heat and leave the syrup to cool. Pour the syrup through a tea strainer into a jug. Throw away the rind left in the tea strainer.

8. Pour a teaspoon or two of syrup over each cake, until all the syrup is used up. Leave the cakes on the wire rack until they are completely cold.

9. To make the icing, sift the icing sugar into a bowl. Put the butter and three tablespoons of juice into a small pan. Gently heat the pan until the butter has melted.

10. Pour the melted mixture over the icing sugar. Stir it to make a smooth, glossy icing. Spread the icing over the cakes. Decorate each cake with lemon and lime rind.

Mocha butterfly cakes

The combination of chocolate and coffee is known as mocha. These mocha butterfly cakes are filled with vanilla buttercream and dusted with icing sugar.

Ingredients:

Makes 12

For the cakes:
100g (4oz) butter, softened
100g (4oz) soft light brown sugar
2 medium eggs
1½ teaspoons coffee powder or
    granules
1 teaspoon warm water
75g (3oz) self-raising flour
25g (1oz) cocoa powder

For the vanilla buttercream:
40g (1½oz) butter, softened
1 teaspoon vanilla essence
75g (3oz) icing sugar

a 12-hole shallow bun tray
paper cake cases

1. Heat the oven to 180°C, 350°F, gas mark 4. Put the butter and sugar in a large bowl. Beat them with a wooden spoon until the mixture is light and fluffy.

2. Break the eggs into a small bowl and beat them with a fork. Put the coffee powder into a cup with the warm water. Stir them together and add them to the eggs.

3. Pour the eggy mixture into the large bowl, a little at a time, beating well after each addition. Sift the flour and cocoa over it. Fold in the flour until it is smooth.

4. Put a paper case into each hole in the tray. Use a teaspoon to spoon the mixture into each paper case. Use another teaspoon to help you scrape the mixture off.

5. Bake the cakes in the oven for 15 minutes, until they are firm. Take them out of the oven. Leave them in the tray for five minutes, then lift them onto a wire rack.

6. Using a sharp knife, carefully cut a circle from the top of each cake. Cut each circle in half, across the middle. Use the recipe on page 75 to make the vanilla buttercream.

7. Spread some buttercream onto each cake. Then, gently push two of the half slices into the icing, so that they look like butterfly wings. Sift a little icing sugar over the top.

Chef's Tip

Instead of butterfly cakes, you could make 'top hat' cakes. Just press the circle you cut from the cake, straight onto the buttercream, without cutting it.

41

Mint choc chip cakes

These tiny chocolate chip cakes are topped with a delicious minty icing and decorated with more chocolate chips.

Ingredients:

Makes about 25 cakes

40g (1½oz) caster sugar
40g (1½oz) soft margarine
40g (1½oz) self-raising flour
1 tablespoon cocoa powder
1 medium egg
1 tablespoon plain chocolate drops
1 tablespoon white chocolate drops

For the peppermint icing:
175g (6oz) icing sugar
1½ tablespoons warm water
1 teaspoon peppermint essence
2 drops green food dye

chocolate drops for decorating

small paper cases

Chef's Tip

Always add food dye to a mixture a little at a time. Try pouring some onto a teaspoon first. If you pour out too much, you can tip some away.

1. Heat the oven to 180°C, 350°F, gas mark 4. Arrange 25 small paper cases on a baking tray. Put the sugar and margarine into a large mixing bowl.

2. Sift the flour and cocoa powder into the bowl. Break the egg into a cup, then add it to the bowl. Stir all the ingredients together until the mixture is smooth and creamy.

3. Spoon half the mixture into another bowl. Add the plain chocolate drops to one bowl and the white chocolate drops to the other bowl and stir them in.

Fill each case until it is just under half full.

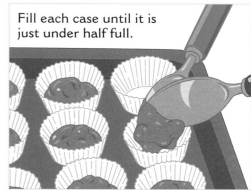

4. Using a teaspoon, spoon all the mixture into the paper cases. Bake the cakes for 12 minutes, until they are firm. Wear oven gloves to take them out of the oven.

5. Lift the cakes onto a wire rack to cool. For the icing, sift the icing sugar into a bowl. Add the warm water, peppermint essence and the green food dye.

6. Stir the icing until it is smooth. Use a teaspoon to spread a little icing onto each cake. Decorate the cakes with plain and white chocolate drops.

Try decorating the cakes with different types of chocolate. See page 73 to make chocolate curls.

Lemon and berry muffins

Lemons and fresh berries are the main ingredients in these delicious, light muffins. They work well with blackberries, blueberries or raspberries.

For a special occasion or a gift, you could tie card and ribbon around your muffins.

Ingredients:

Makes 12 muffins

1 lemon
250g (9oz) self-raising flour
1 teaspoon bicarbonate of soda
150g (5oz) caster sugar
90ml (3½fl oz) sunflower oil
150g (5oz) carton low fat
  lemon flavoured yogurt
2 medium eggs
150g (5oz) fresh berries
75g (3oz) icing sugar

a 12-hole muffin or deep bun tray
paper muffin cases

1. Put a muffin case into each hole in the tray. Heat the oven to 190°C, 375°F, gas mark 5. Use the medium holes of a grater to grate the zest of the lemon onto a small plate.

2. Sift the flour and bicarbonate of soda into a large mixing bowl and stir in the caster sugar. Make a hollow in the middle of the mixture with a spoon.

3. Measure the oil into a jug. Add the lemon yogurt and the zest. Cut the lemon in half and squeeze out the juice from one half. Add the lemon juice to the oily mixture.

4. Break the eggs into a small bowl and beat them well. Add them to the oily mixture too. Use a metal spoon to mix the ingredients until they are well blended.

5. Pour the oily mixture into the hollow in the dry ingredients. Stir all the ingredients for a few seconds. Add the berries, then gently stir everything together.

Chef's Tip

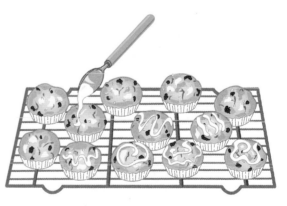

The secret of really light muffins is not to stir the mixture too much. It should look a bit lumpy when you spoon it into the paper cases.

6. Spoon the mixture into the paper cases. Fill each one almost to the top. Bake the muffins for 15-18 minutes, until they are golden and firm to touch.

7. Leave the muffins in the tray for five minutes. Lift them onto a wire rack. Sift some icing sugar over them. To make lemon icing to drizzle over them, see page 53.

Fudgy banana muffins

Chunks of fudge melt into these muffins and give them a lovely, moist texture. They are delicious topped with honey and eaten while they are still warm.

Ingredients:

Makes 12 muffins

250g (9oz) self-raising flour
1 teaspoon baking powder
100g (4oz) fudge
100g (4oz) soft light brown sugar
75g (3oz) butter
125ml (4½fl oz) milk
1 teaspoon vanilla essence
2 medium ripe bananas
2 medium eggs

2 tablespoons clear honey

a 12-hole muffin or deep bun tray
paper muffin cases

1. Heat the oven to 190°C, 375°F, gas mark 5. Put a paper muffin case into each hole in a muffin tray. Sift the flour and baking powder into a large mixing bowl.

2. Put the fudge on a chopping board and cut it into chunks. Add the sugar and fudge to the bowl and stir them in. Make a hollow in the middle of the mixture.

3. Put the butter in a saucepan. Heat it gently over a low heat until the butter has melted. Remove the pan from the heat and add the milk and vanilla essence.

4. Peel the bananas and put them into a small bowl. Mash them with a fork until they are fairly smooth. Break the eggs into another bowl and beat them with a fork.

5. Add the bananas and the beaten eggs to the pan. Stir the ingredients in the pan. Then, pour the mixture into the hollow in the dry ingredients.

Fill each paper case almost to the top.

6. Stir everything with a wooden spoon, until it is just mixed together. The mixture should still look quite lumpy. Then, spoon it into the paper cases.

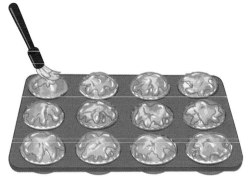

7. Bake the muffins for 20 minutes, until they are firm and well-risen. Leave them in the tray for five minutes. Brush the tops with honey, then lift them onto a wire rack.

Chocolate fudge brownies

Delicious served slightly warm, these brownies have a crisp, sugary top and a gooey centre. Traditionally, brownies contain lots of pecans or walnuts, but you can use dried cranberries or other types of nuts if you like.

Ingredients:

Makes 9 squares

100g (4oz) plain chocolate drops
2 large eggs
125g (5oz) butter, softened
275g (10oz) caster sugar
½ teaspoon vanilla essence
50g (2oz) self-raising flour
25g (1oz) plain flour
2 tablespoons cocoa powder
100g (4oz) walnuts or pecans

a 20cm (8in) square cake tin, at least 6½cm (2½in) deep

Chef's Tip

When you melt chocolate, make sure that the bowl and the spoon are dry. Even one drop of water can make the chocolate go dry and lumpy.

Cut just inside the line.

1. Heat the oven to 180°C, 350°F, gas mark 4. Put the tin on a piece of baking parchment and draw around it with a pencil. Then, cut out the square of parchment.

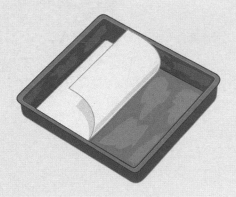

2. Use a paper towel to wipe a little oil over the insides of the tin. Put the square of paper inside the tin. Then, pour about 5cm (2in) of water into a pan and heat it.

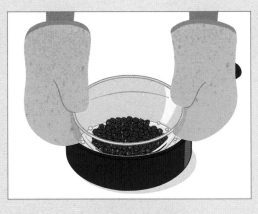

3. When the water bubbles, remove the pan from the heat. Put the chocolate drops into a heatproof bowl. Carefully, put the bowl inside the pan.

4. Stir the chocolate drops until they have melted, then wearing oven gloves, carefully lift the bowl out of the pan. Break the eggs into a small bowl and beat them.

5. Put the butter, sugar and vanilla essence in a large mixing bowl. Beat them until they are fluffy. Add the eggs, a little at a time, beating between each addition.

6. Sift both types of flour and the cocoa powder into the bowl. Add the melted chocolate and stir all the ingredients together until they are well-mixed.

7. Put the nuts on a chopping board. Cut them into small pieces. Stir them into the mixture. Spoon the mixture into the tin. Smooth the top with the back of a spoon.

8. Bake the brownies for 35 minutes. They are ready when they have risen slightly and a crust has formed on top, but they will still be soft in the middle.

9. Leave the brownies in the tin for 20 minutes. Then, cut them into squares. If you want to stencil an icing sugar design on top, find out how on page 73.

Strawberry shortcake

Strawberry shortcake is made up from layers of sweet scone, cream and strawberries. Put the layers together just before you eat the shortcake.

Ingredients:

Serves 8

For the shortcake:
225g (8oz) self-raising flour
1 teaspoon baking powder
50g (2oz) butter or margarine
25g (1oz) caster sugar
1 medium egg
5 tablespoons milk
½ teaspoon vanilla essence
extra milk, for brushing

For the filling:
225g (8oz) strawberries
150ml (¼ pint) double or
   whipping cream
3 tablespoons Greek yogurt
icing sugar

Use a sieve.

1. Heat the oven to 220°C, 425°F, gas mark 7. Use a paper towel to wipe some cooking oil over a baking tray. Sift the flour and baking powder into a large bowl.

2. Cut the butter into small cubes. Add the cubes to the flour, then rub them in with the tips of your fingers. Carry on until the mixture looks like fine breadcrumbs.

Cut the strawberries in half lengthways to decorate the top of the cake.

3. Stir in the caster sugar and make a hollow in the middle of the mixture with a spoon. Then, break the egg into a cup and stir it with a fork, to mix the white and yolk.

4. Stir the milk and vanilla into the egg, then pour the mixture into the hollow in the flour. Mix all the ingredients with a blunt knife, to make a soft dough.

5. Sprinkle a clean work surface with a little flour, then shape the dough into a ball with your hands. Squash the ball a little, then put it onto the work surface.

Cut out the stalks before you slice the strawberries.

Cut the shortcake like this.

6. Using a rolling pin, roll out the dough to make a circle shape which is about 20cm (8in) across. Lift it onto the baking tray and brush it with a little milk.

7. Bake the shortcake in the oven for 12-15 minutes, until it has risen and is golden brown. Rinse and dry the strawberries, then cut them into thick slices.

Put the shortcake on a plate.

8. Take the shortcake out of the oven and slide it onto a wire rack, to cool. When the shortcake is cool, very carefully cut it in half horizontally, with a bread knife.

9. Lift the top layer onto a chopping board and cut it into eight wedges. Then, pour the cream into a bowl. Whisk it until it is thick, then mix in the yogurt.

10. Using a blunt knife, spread half of the creamy mixture over the bottom half of the shortcake. Then, lay the strawberry slices all over the top of it.

11. Spread the rest of the cream mixture over the strawberries. Lay the eight shortcake wedges on the top. Sift icing sugar over the top of the shortcake.

Lemon layer cake

Layers of lemon cake are sandwiched together with home-made lemon curd, then topped with a tangy lemon icing.

Ingredients:

Makes 10 slices

1 lemon
225g (8oz) self-raising flour
1 teaspoon baking powder
4 medium eggs
225g (8oz) soft margarine
225g (8oz) caster sugar

For the lemon curd filling:
2 medium eggs
75g (3oz) caster sugar
1 lemon
50g (2oz) unsalted butter

For the lemon icing:
1 lemon
125g (5oz) icing sugar

three 20cm (8in) round,
    shallow cake tins

1. Heat the oven to 180°C, 350°F, gas mark 4. Grease and line three tins. Use a grater to grate the rind of a lemon. Cut the lemon in half and squeeze out the juice.

2. Sift the flour and baking powder into a bowl. Break the eggs into a cup, then add them, along with the margarine and sugar. Beat everything together well.

3. Stir in the lemon juice and rind. Divide the mixture between the tins. Bake the cakes for 20 minutes, until they are firm. Then, turn them out onto a wire rack to cool.

4. To make the lemon curd, break the eggs into a heatproof bowl and beat them with a fork. Add the sugar. Grate the rind of the lemon and squeeze out the juice.

5. Add the rind and juice to the bowl. Cut the butter into chunks and add it, too. Put 5cm (2in) water into a pan. Heat it until it is just bubbling. Put the bowl into the pan.

6. Stir the mixture with a wooden spoon as it thickens. After about 20 minutes, the mixture should coat the back of a metal spoon. Take the pan off the heat.

Don't worry if some filling oozes out.

7. Spread one of the cakes with half of the lemon curd. Put another cake on top. Spread the rest of curd over that cake. Then, put the final cake on top.

8. Grate the rind of the remaining lemon, or scrape some off with a zester. Keep the rind to one side. For the lemon icing, sift the icing sugar into a bowl.

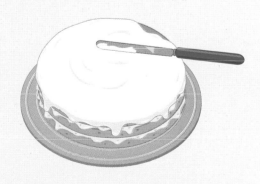

9. Squeeze the juice from one half of the lemon. Stir the juice into the icing until it is smooth. Spread the icing over the cake. Sprinkle the rind on top of the cake.

Rich chocolate cake

This dark, moist cake is very rich, so serve it in thin slices. Drizzle it with chocolate glaze and scatter fresh berries on top.

Ingredients:

Makes 12 slices

For the cake:
150g (5oz) plain chocolate drops
75g (3oz) butter, softened
4 medium eggs
100g (4oz) caster sugar
30g (1oz) self-raising flour

For the chocolate glaze:
175g (6oz) plain chocolate drops
150ml (¼ pint) double cream
1½ tablespoons golden syrup
225g (8oz) fresh berries

a 20cm (8in) round cake tin,
    at least 7½cm (3in) deep

1. Heat the oven to 180°C, 350°F or gas mark 4. Use a paper towel to wipe the insides of the tin with cooking oil. Put the tin on some baking parchment. Draw around it.

2. Cut out the circle of paper and lay it inside the tin. Pour 5cm (2in) water into a large saucepan and heat it. When the water bubbles, remove the pan from the heat.

Wear oven gloves to lift the bowl out of the pan.

The egg whites should make stiff peaks, like this, when you lift the whisk.

3. Put the chocolate drops and butter into a large heatproof bowl. Put the bowl into the pan. Stir the mixture until it has melted, then take the bowl out of the pan.

4. Break an egg onto a plate. Cover the yolk with an egg cup. Hold the egg cup and tip the plate so the egg white slides off into another bowl. Put the yolk into a cup.

5. Do the same with the other eggs until all the whites are in one bowl and the yolks are in the cup. Whisk the egg whites with a whisk until they are really thick.

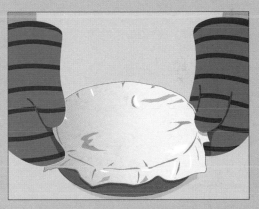

6. Add the egg yolks and sugar to the melted butter and chocolate. Stir them in. Sift the flour over the mixture and stir that in too. Then, add the whisked egg whites.

7. Gently fold in the egg whites with a metal spoon. Pour the mixture into the tin and bake it in the oven. After 20 minutes, take the cake out of the oven.

8. Cover the cake with tin foil to stop the top of it from burning. Put it back in the oven for another 15-20 minutes. When the cake is firm, take it out of the oven.

Peel off the baking parchment.

9. Leave the cake in the tin to cool for 20 minutes. Run the knife around the sides of the tin. Turn it upside down over a wire rack and shake it so the cake pops out.

10. For the chocolate glaze, put the chocolate drops, cream and syrup into a small pan. Gently heat the pan and stir the mixture until all the ingredients have melted.

11. Spoon some chocolate glaze over the top of the cake so it drizzles down the sides. Arrange fresh berries on top of the cake to decorate it.

Carrot cake

This is a light, moist cake, with a spicy flavour. It is covered with a lemon flavoured cream cheese topping.

Ingredients:

Makes 12 slices

For the cake:
2 medium carrots
3 medium eggs
175ml (6fl oz) sunflower oil
200g (7oz) caster sugar
100g (4oz) chopped pecans
   or walnuts
200g (7oz) plain flour
1½ teaspoons baking powder
1½ teaspoons bicarbonate of soda
1½ teaspoons ground cinnamon
1 teaspoon ground ginger
½ teaspoon salt

For the topping:
50g (2oz) icing sugar
200g (7oz) full fat cream cheese,
   at room temperature
1 tablespoon lemon juice
½ teaspoon vanilla essence
pecan or walnut halves to
   decorate

a 27 x 18cm (7 x 11in)
   rectangular, shallow cake tin

1. Heat the oven to 180°C, 350°F, gas mark 4. Grease the tin with some cooking oil on a paper towel. Put the tin on some baking parchment and draw around it.

2. Cut out the rectangle and lay it in the tin. Wash the carrots and cut off their tops. Hold each carrot firmly and carefully grate it on the biggest holes of a grater.

3. Crack the eggs into a small bowl and beat them with a fork. Put the sunflower oil and sugar into a larger bowl and beat them for a minute with a wooden spoon.

4. Add the beaten eggs to the larger bowl, a little at a time. Beat the mixture well after each addition. Then, stir in the grated carrots and the chopped nuts.

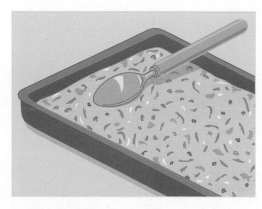

5. Sift the flour, baking powder, bicarbonate of soda, cinnamon, ginger and salt over the mixture. Gently fold everything together with a metal spoon.

6. Spoon the mixture into the tin. Use the back of a spoon to smooth the top of the mixture. Bake the cake for 45 minutes until it is well-risen and firm.

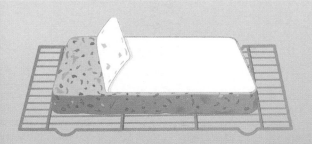

7. Leave the cake in the tin for ten minutes to cool. Run a knife around the sides of the cake. Carefully turn the cake out onto a wire rack. Peel off the parchment.

8. Sift the icing sugar into a bowl. Add the cream cheese, lemon juice and vanilla. Beat the mixture well. When the cake has cooled, spoon the topping onto it.

9. Spread the topping over the cake with a blunt knife, making lots of swirly patterns. Then, decorate the cake with pecan or walnut halves, or lemon rind.

Chocolate log

Sift more icing sugar over the log before you serve it.

Chocolate log cakes are sometimes known as yule logs and are made at Christmas-time. You can fill this chocolate log with cherries and cream or the raspberry cream, which is on page 74.

Ingredients:

Makes about 10 slices

For the cake:
4 large eggs
125g (5oz) caster sugar
60g (2½oz) ground almonds
1½ tablespoons cocoa powder
1¼ teaspoons baking powder

For the filling:
300ml (½ pint) double cream
1 tin of cherries

a 35 x 25cm (14 x 10in) Swiss roll tin

1. Heat the oven to 180°C, 350°F, gas mark 4. Grease and line the tin. Separate all the eggs so the whites are in one bowl and the yolks are in another bowl.

2. Add the sugar to the yolks. Whisk them together with a fork, until the mixture is pale and thick. Stir in the ground almonds, cocoa powder and baking powder.

3. Whisk the egg whites with a whisk, until they are really thick. When you lift the whisk up, the egg whites should make stiff peaks, like this.

4. Spoon the egg whites into the mixture. Gently fold them in with a metal spoon. When all the ingredients are well-mixed, pour the mixture into the tin.

5. Bake the cake in the oven for 20-25 minutes, until it is firm and springy. Leave it in the tin for ten minutes to cool. Then, cover it with baking parchment and a cloth.

6. Put the tin in the fridge for at least two hours to chill. Meanwhile, pour the double cream into a bowl. Use a whisk to whisk the cream until it is just thick.

7. Take the cake out of the fridge. Run a knife around the sides to loosen the edges. Lay a sheet of baking parchment on a work surface. Sift icing sugar onto it.

8. Turn the cake onto the baking parchment. Peel off the oily parchment. Spread the cream over the cake. Use a sieve to drain the syrup from the cherries.

Use the parchment to help you roll up the cake.

9. Remove the cherry stones and scatter the cherries over the cream. Carefully, roll up the cake from one of the short ends. Then, lift the cake onto a plate.

Tropical fruit loaf

You can make this fruit loaf with a packet of ready-chopped tropical fruits, such as pineapple, mango and papaya. You can make it from your own choice of dried fruits, if you prefer, such as apricots, cherries or figs, but keep the total weight of the fruit the same.

Ingredients:

Makes about 10 slices

For the loaf:
1 large orange
175g (6oz) butter, softened
175g (6oz) caster sugar
3 medium eggs
100g (4oz) self-raising
    wholemeal flour
100g (4oz) plain flour
1 teaspoon baking powder
250g (9oz) packet chopped
    dried tropical fruit

For the orange icing:
75g (3oz) icing sugar

a 900g (2lb) loaf tin, measuring
    about 20½ x 12½ x 8cm
    (8 x 5 x 3½in)

1. Heat the oven to 180°C, 350°F, gas mark 4. Grease the tin and line it with baking parchment. Grate the rind of the orange, using the medium holes of a grater.

2. Cut the orange in half and squeeze out the juice. Pour the juice into a jug. Put the rind, butter and sugar into a large bowl. Beat them until they are creamy.

3. Break the eggs into a small bowl and beat them with a fork. Add them to the creamy mixture, a little at a time. Sift both flours and the baking powder into the bowl.

Smooth the top of the mixture with the back of a spoon.

Wear oven gloves to take the cake out of the oven.

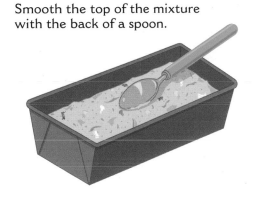

4. Chop the tropical fruit into small pieces. Set aside 25g (1oz) of the fruit. Then, add the rest to the mixture, with a tablespoon of the orange juice.

5. Gently fold the ingredients together with a metal spoon until they are well-mixed. Spoon the mixture into the tin. Then, put the cake into the oven for 20 minutes.

6. Take the cake out of the oven. Cover the tin with foil to stop the cake from burning. Put the cake back in the oven for a further 50 minutes, then take it out again.

Peel off the baking parchment.

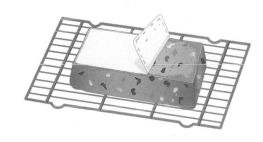

7. Press the cake with a finger. If it feels firm, leave it in the tin for 15 minutes to cool, then turn it onto a wire rack. If it isn't firm, put it back in the oven to cook until it is firm.

8. Sift the icing sugar into a bowl. Stir in a tablespoon of the orange juice. Use a blunt knife to spread the icing over the cake. Then, scatter the remaining fruit on top.

Chocolate orange cake

Chocolate and orange taste delicious together. Wholemeal flour makes this cake crunchy around the edges, while the yogurt makes it light in the middle.

Ingredients:

Serves 8

1 medium orange
175g (6oz) soft margarine
175g (6oz) caster sugar
3 medium eggs
2 tablespoons cocoa powder
2 tablespoons warm water
1 teaspoon baking powder
200g (7oz) self-raising wholemeal flour
5 tablespoons plain natural yogurt

For the icing:
100g (4oz) milk chocolate drops
175g (6oz) plain chocolate drops
150ml (¼ pint) soured cream

a 20cm (8in) round cake tin, at least 7½cm (3in) deep

Decorate your cake with chocolate curls (see page 73 for how to make them).

1. Heat the oven to 170°C, 325°F, gas mark 3. Pour a little cooking oil into the tin and wipe it over the insides. Put the tin on some baking parchment and draw around it.

2. Cut out the circle and lay it in the tin. Grate the rind of the orange, using the medium holes of the grater. Cut the orange in half and squeeze out the juice.

Beat the mixture with a wooden spoon.

3. Put the margarine into a large mixing bowl. Beat it until it is soft and smooth. Stir in the sugar and orange rind. Beat the mixture until it is light and fluffy.

4. Crack the eggs into a small bowl and beat them well with a fork. Pour the eggs into the large mixing bowl, a little at a time. Beat the mixture well after each addition.

5. Put the cocoa powder into a small bowl. Stir in the warm water to make a smooth paste. Then, add the paste to the mixture in the large bowl and stir it in.

Smooth the top of the mixture with the back of a spoon.

6. Use a sieve to sift the baking powder and about half of the flour over the mixture. Then, add half of the yogurt. Gently fold the ingredients together.

7. Sift the remaining flour into the bowl. Tip any bran left in the sieve into the bowl too. Add the rest of the yogurt and fold it in. Add the orange juice and fold it in too.

8. Spoon the mixture into the tin. Bake the cake for one hour. Take it out of the oven and press it with your finger. If the cake feels firm, leave it in the tin to cool.

Peel the baking parchment off the cake.

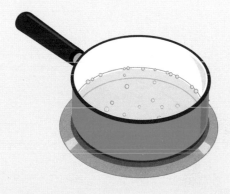

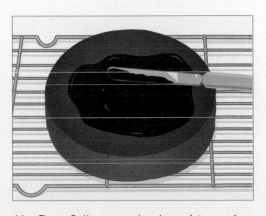

9. If the cake isn't firm, put it back in the oven to cook until it is firm. Then, run a knife around the sides of the tin. Turn out the cake onto a wire rack to cool.

10. For the icing, pour 5cm (2in) of water into a pan. Heat it until the water bubbles. Remove the pan from the heat. Put the chocolate drops into a heatproof bowl.

11. Carefully, put the bowl into the pan. Stir the chocolate until it melts. Take the bowl out of the pan. Whisk in the soured cream. When it is cool, spread it over the cake.

Raspberry and almond cake

This sponge cake is filled with fresh raspberries and jam. It is light and fluffy because it is made from ground almonds instead of flour and butter.

Ingredients:

Makes 10 slices

For the cake:
4 medium eggs
165g (5½oz) caster sugar
225g (8oz) ground almonds
1 teaspoon baking powder

For the filling:
150g (5oz) seedless raspberry jam
150g (5oz) fresh raspberries

For the icing:
200g (7oz) icing sugar
2 tablespoons warm water
a handful of raspberries to
    decorate

a 20cm (8in) round cake tin,
    about 7½cm (3in) deep

Chef's Tip

Cutting a cake in half horizontally can be quite tricky. If you prefer, you can spread the filling over the top of the cake instead, and serve it as a pudding.

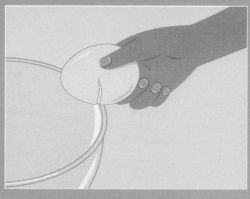

1. Heat the oven to 170°C, 325°F or gas mark 3. Grease and line the tin. Break one egg on the edge of a bowl. Pour it onto a small plate. Put an egg cup over the yolk.

3. Add the sugar to the yolks. Use a fork to beat them together until they are a slightly paler colour. Use a whisk to whisk the egg whites until they are stiff.

Smooth the top of the mixture with the back of a spoon.

5. Add the almonds and baking powder. Fold everything together until it is well-mixed. Pour the mixture into the tin and bake it in the oven for 35-40 minutes.

2. Hold the egg cup and tip the plate over a bowl, so the egg white dribbles into it. Do the same with all the eggs, so the whites are in one bowl and the yolks in another.

4. When you lift the whisk, the egg whites should form stiff peaks. Add the whites to the yolk mixture. Using a metal spoon, gently fold them into the mixture.

Peel the baking parchment off the cake.

6. Leave the cake in the tin for 20 minutes. Run a knife around the sides of the tin. Turn the tin upside down over a wire rack and shake it so the cake pops out.

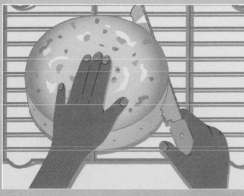

7. To cut the cake in half horizontally, put your hand on top of the cake to keep it steady. Then, using a bread knife, carefully cut the cake in half.

8. For the filling, put the jam in a small bowl and beat it. Mix in the raspberries. Spread the filling over the bottom half of the cake. Carefully replace the top half.

9. Sift the icing sugar into a bowl. Add the water and stir it in to make a smooth paste. Use a blunt knife to spread the icing over the cake. Scatter raspberries on top.

Cherry crumble cake

This cake has a crunchy, crumbly top, with streaks of jam inside. You can use any type of jam, but brightly-coloured ones look more fun.

Ingredients:

Makes 12 slices

For the topping:
75g (3oz) plain flour
25g (1oz) porridge oats
25g (1oz) sunflower seeds
75g (3oz) soft light brown sugar
50g (2oz) butter

For the sponge:
200g (7oz) self-raising flour
1 teaspoon cinnamon
½ teaspoon baking powder
pinch of salt
125g (4½oz) caster sugar
40g (1½oz) butter
2 large eggs
200ml (7fl oz) soured cream
375g (15oz) red cherry jam

a 27 x 18cm (11 x 7in)
    rectangular cake tin, at least
    4cm (1¾in) deep

66

1. Heat the oven to 180°C, 350°F, gas mark 4. Grease and line the tin. For the topping, sift the flour into a large mixing bowl. Stir in the oats, seeds and sugar.

2. Put the butter in a saucepan and heat it until it has just melted. Remove the pan from the heat. Carefully, pour the butter over the ingredients in the bowl.

3. Use a fork to stir together the ingredients in the bowl. Then, put the bowl into the fridge to chill, while you make the mixture for the sponge.

4. Sift the flour, cinnamon, baking powder and salt into another large bowl. Stir in the sugar. Heat the butter in a saucepan. When it has just melted, pour it into a jug.

5. Crack the eggs into a small bowl and beat them with a fork. When the butter in the jug has cooled, add the eggs and the soured cream. Stir them together.

6. Pour the mixture from the jug into the dry ingredients. Beat everything together with a wooden spoon until it is smooth. Spoon the mixture into the tin.

  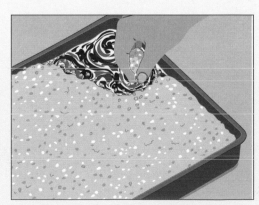

Make sure the jam is pushed down into the cake.

7. Use a spoon to push the mixture into the corners of the tin. Put the jam into a bowl and beat it with a fork. Then, use a teaspoon to drop jam on top of the cake.

8. When the top of the cake is almost covered with jam, swirl the jam through the mixture with a knife. This will make a marbled pattern when the cake is cooked.

9. Take the topping out of the fridge. Break it up and sprinkle it evenly over the cake. Bake the cake for 40 minutes. Leave it in the tin to cool before you serve it.

Lemon ricotta cake

This lemony cake contains ricotta, a mild Italian cheese made from sheep's milk. To make this marbled topping, you sprinkle plain and white chocolate drops over the cake while it is still warm, so they melt. Then, you swirl them together.

Ingredients:

Makes 9 squares

2 lemons
3 eggs
50g (2oz) butter, softened
300g (10oz) caster sugar
250g (9oz) tub ricotta cheese
175g (6oz) self-raising flour
50g (2oz) white chocolate drops
25g (1oz) plain chocolate drops

a 20cm (8in) square cake tin,
    at least 6½cm (2½in) deep

1. Grease the tin and line it with baking parchment. Heat the oven to 180°C, 350°F, gas mark 4. Grate the rind of the lemons using the smallest holes of a grater.

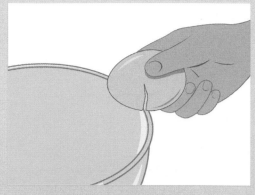

2. To separate the egg white from the yolk, carefully break one egg on the edge of a cup or bowl. Slide the egg slowly onto a plate. Put an egg cup over the yolk.

Save the yolks in a cup.

3. Holding the egg cup, tip the plate over another bowl, so that the egg white dribbles into it. Do the same with the other eggs, so that all the whites are in the bowl.

4. Whisk the egg whites with a whisk until they are really thick. When you lift the whisk up, the egg whites should make stiff peaks, like this.

5. Put the butter, sugar, egg yolks and lemon rind into another large bowl. Beat them together with a fork. Add the ricotta, a spoonful at a time, beating after each addition.

6. Sift the flour over the mixture. Gently fold it in with a metal spoon. Add the egg whites and fold these in too. Then, spoon the mixture into the cake tin.

7. Smooth the top of the mixture with the back of a spoon. Bake the cake in the oven for 45-50 minutes, until it feels firm when you touch it.

8. While the cake is still hot, sprinkle the white chocolate drops over the top. Then, scatter the plain chocolate drops. Leave the chocolate to melt for five minutes.

9. Use a teaspoon to swirl the chocolate into a marbled pattern. Leave the cake until the topping is dry. Run a knife around the sides of the cake, then cut it into squares.

Blueberry cheesecake

This baked cheesecake is made from cream cheese, eggs and double cream. It has a rich, velvety texture, which goes well with juicy blueberries or other berries. Chill it well before you eat it.

Ingredients:

Serves 10

175g (6oz) digestive biscuits
75g (3oz) butter
1 tablespoon demerara sugar
1 lemon
350g (12oz) full fat cream cheese
100g (4oz) caster sugar
3 medium eggs
1 tablespoon cornflour
150ml (¼ pint) whipping cream
150g (5oz) fresh blueberries

For the topping:
4 tablespoons blueberry or
    raspberry jam
150g (5oz) fresh berries
fresh mint

a 20cm (8in) spring-clip tin with
    a loose base, at least 6½cm
    (2½in) deep

Chef's Tip

Always use full fat cream cheese, as low fat cheese will curdle when it is cooked. You could also make this cheesecake with raspberries instead of blueberries.

1. Heat the oven to 150°C, 300°F, gas mark 2. Wipe a little oil over the insides of the tin with a paper towel. Then, put the digestive biscuits into a clean plastic bag.

3. Put the butter and demerara sugar into a saucepan. Heat it over low heat until the butter has melted. Lift the pan off the heat and stir in the biscuit crumbs.

5. Grate the rind of the lemon on the medium holes of a grater. Then, cut the lemon in half and squeeze the juice from it, using a lemon squeezer.

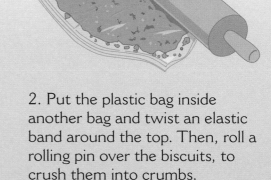

2. Put the plastic bag inside another bag and twist an elastic band around the top. Then, roll a rolling pin over the biscuits, to crush them into crumbs.

4. Spoon the mixture into the pan and spread it out. Press it down with the back of a spoon, to make a firm, flat base. Bake the biscuit base in the oven for 15 minutes.

6. Put the cream cheese, sugar, lemon rind and juice into a large bowl. Stir them together. To separate the eggs, break one on the edge of a bowl. Pour it onto a plate.

7. Hold an egg cup over the yolk. Tip the plate over a clean bowl, so the egg white dribbles into it. Put the yolk in another bowl. Separate all the eggs in the same way.

8. Add the egg yolks to the cream cheese mixture. Add the cornflour and cream. Mix everything together until it is smooth. Then, stir in the blueberries.

9. Whisk the egg whites with a whisk until they are really thick. When you lift the whisk up, the egg whites should make stiff peaks, like this.

10. Add the egg whites to the mixture. Gently fold them in with a metal spoon. Then, pour the mixture over the base and bake it for 50 minutes. Turn off the oven.

11. Leave the cheesecake in the oven for one hour. Then take the cheesecake out of the tin and leave it to cool. While it is cooling, make the topping.

12. Put the jam in a pan with two teaspoons of water. Heat the pan until the jam has melted. Spoon it over the cheescake and sprinkle fresh berries and mint on top.

Decorating ideas

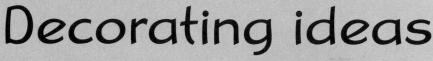

There are lots of different ways to decorate your cakes and biscuits. You could try out different colours of icing and add piped icing, sweets, sprinkles, sugar flowers or chocolate curls. You could also make patterns with sugar sifted over a stencil.

Piping icing

175g (6oz) icing sugar
1½ tablespoons warm water
coloured food dye

To pipe the icing:
two small plastic food bags

You can stick sweets to plain cakes with a dot of icing.

Use a blunt knife to spread on the icing.

1. Sift the icing sugar into a bowl. Stir in the warm water to make smooth paste. Spread half of the icing over the cake.

2. Add two drops of food dye to the icing in the bowl and mix it in well. Put one plastic food bag inside the other.

3. Spoon the blue icing into the bag. Hold it over the bowl and snip off a tiny corner. Be careful that the icing doesn't run out.

4. Move the bag over the cake, taking care not to spill. Gently squeeze the bag as you draw patterns on the cake.

Home-made sugar sprinkles

1. Put one tablespoon of caster sugar in a bowl. Add one drop of food dye and mix it in. Spread it onto a plate to dry.

2. Scoop up the sugar with a spoon and sprinkle it onto an iced cake. You could sprinkle it over a stencil (see below).

Stencil patterns

1. Take a piece of paper that's bigger than your cake. Fold it in half. Draw half of a shape against the fold. Cut it out.

2. Unfold the paper and lay it on your cake. Sift cocoa over a light cake or icing sugar over a dark cake. Take off the paper.

Chocolate curls

1. Take a bar of cooking chocolate. Use a vegetable peeler to scrape chocolate from the side of the bar.

2. Keep scraping to shave off little curls. To make bigger curls, scrape the chocolate from underneath the bar.

To stencil onto an iced cake, wait for the icing to dry first.

Chocolate will curl better when it is at room temperature and not too cold.

Creams and fillings

Here are some ideas for different creams and fillings you could use with a Victoria sponge or some of the other cakes in this book.

Whisking cream

Stand the bowl on a damp cloth, to stop it from slipping.

1. Pour 200ml (7fl oz) whipping cream into a bowl. Hold the bowl and twist the whisk around and around very quickly.

2. Whisk the cream until it starts to form stiff peaks when you lift the whisk, but stop before it becomes too solid.

Vanilla cream

For vanilla cream, add ½ teaspoon of vanilla essence and sift over one tablespoon of icing sugar, before whipping the cream.

Raspberry cream

For raspberry cream, mash 150g (6oz) fresh raspberries with a fork. Stir them into the whipped cream with 1½ tablespoons of caster sugar.

Lime cream

1 lime
250g (9oz) mascarpone
25g (1oz) icing sugar

You could also try adding the grated rind of an orange or lemon instead of a lime.

1. Using the small holes of a grater, grate the rind of the lime. Put the rind in a mixing bowl with the mascarpone.

2. Sift over the icing sugar. Mix everything together until the mascarpone is smooth and has green flecks all the way through.

Try filling a chocolate log with raspberry cream.

Buttercream

This recipe makes enough buttercream to sandwich together two sponge cakes. To cover the cake too, double the quantities.

100g (4oz) unsalted butter, softened
225g (8oz) icing sugar
1 tablespoon milk
½ teaspoon vanilla essence

1. Put the butter into a large mixing bowl and beat it with a wooden spoon until it becomes soft and creamy.

2. Sift about one third of the icing sugar over the butter and stir it in. Sift the remaining icing sugar over the mixture.

3. Add the milk and the vanilla essence. Then, beat all the ingredients until the buttercream is really pale and fluffy.

For chocolate buttercream, replace the milk with one tablespoon of cocoa mixed with one tablespoon of warm water.

For coffee buttercream, replace the milk with two teaspoons of instant coffee granules mixed with one tablespoon of water.

For orange buttercream, replace the vanilla and milk with two teaspoons of orange juice and the grated rind of an orange.

Try filling macaroons with orange or chocolate buttercream.

Sweet pastry

On these pages, you can find out how to make sweet, rich shortcrust pastry, which is used to make some of the tarts in this book. You'll also find out how to 'blind' bake a pastry case before filling it. It's much easier to make pastry if your hands are cool. Once you've made it, try not to handle it too much.

'Blind' baking

'Blind' baking means cooking a pastry case for a time with no filling. This helps the pastry to cook more evenly. You line it with kitchen foil and fill it with ceramic baking beans, or dried beans or peas. They stop the pastry bubbling up in the middle.

If you use dried beans or peas, store them in an airtight jar, so that you can use them again and again.

Ingredients:

Makes enough pastry to line a 20cm (8in) flan tin

175g (6oz) plain flour
25g (1oz) icing sugar
100g (4oz) chilled butter
1 medium egg
2 teaspoons cold water

baking beans, or a packet of dried beans or peas

1. Sift the flour and icing sugar through a sieve into a large bowl. Then, cut the butter into cubes and stir them in.

2. Rub the butter into the flour with the tips of your fingers. Carry on rubbing until the mixture looks like fine breadcrumbs.

You will not need the egg white in this recipe.

3. Break the egg onto a saucer. Hold an egg cup over the yolk and tip the saucer over a bowl, so the white dribbles into it.

4. Put the yolk in a small bowl with the water. Mix them with a fork. Then, sprinkle them over the mixture in the large bowl.

5. Stir the mixture until everything starts to stick together. Squeeze the pastry together to make a firm dough.

6. Sprinkle a little flour over a clean work surface. Lift the pastry onto the surface and pat it into a smooth ball.

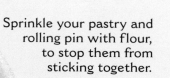

Sprinkle your pastry and rolling pin with flour, to stop them from sticking together.

7. Wrap the pastry in plastic foodwrap. Then, put it into a fridge for 30 minutes. This makes it easier to roll out flat.

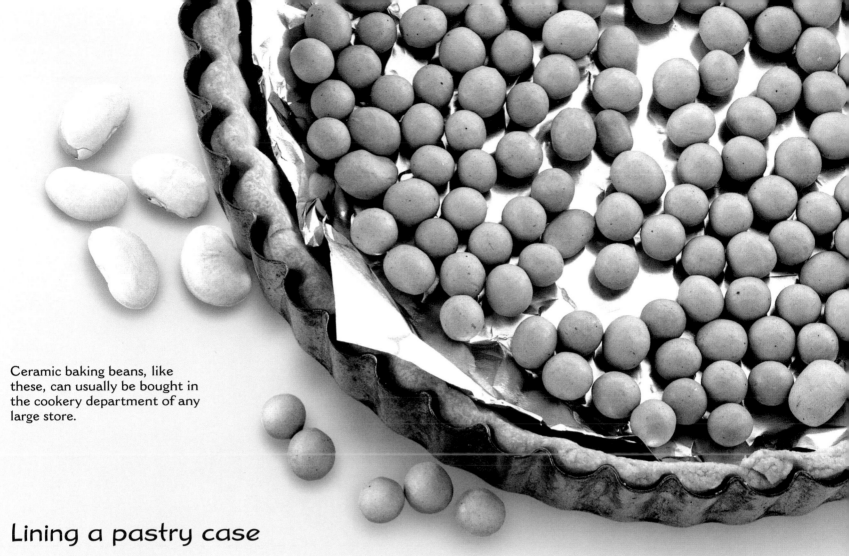

Ceramic baking beans, like these, can usually be bought in the cookery department of any large store.

Lining a pastry case

Turn the pastry a quarter of the way around.

Be careful not to make any holes in the pastry.

The rolling pin cuts off any extra pastry.

1. Put the pastry onto a floury surface. Sprinkle flour onto a rolling pin. Roll over the pastry once, then turn it.

2. Roll over and turn the pastry again and again. Carry on until the pastry is slightly bigger than the flan tin.

3. Roll the pastry around the rolling pin. Lift it up and unroll it over the tin. Gently push the pastry into the edges of the tin.

4. Roll the rolling pin over the tin. Then, cover the pastry case with plastic foodwrap and put it in the fridge for 20 minutes.

'Blind' baking

The holes stop the pastry rising up.

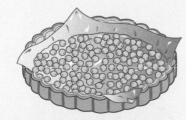

Try not to squash the pastry.

1. Put a baking tray into the oven. Heat the oven to 200°C, 400°F, gas mark 6. Then, prick the pastry base with a fork.

2. Cut a large square of kitchen foil and gently press it into the pastry case. Then, fill the foil with baking beans.

3. Lift out the hot baking tray and put the flan tin on it. Put it back into the oven and bake the pastry case for 8 minutes.

4. Carefully remove the hot foil and beans. Then, bake the empty case for another 5 minutes, or until it is pale golden.

Pear and frangipane tart

Frangipane is a thick mixture of ground almonds, sugar, butter, egg and flour. It rises around the fruit as it cooks, to make a dense, almondy sponge.

Ingredients:

Serves 8

For the pastry:
175g (6oz) plain flour
25g (1oz) icing sugar
100g (4oz) chilled butter
1 medium egg
2 teaspoons cold water

For the frangipane:
50g (2oz) butter, softened
50g (2oz) caster sugar
50g (2oz) ground almonds
1 medium egg
15g (½oz) self-raising flour
3 small, ripe pears

For the glaze:
2 tablespoons smooth apricot jam
1 tablespoon lemon juice

baking beans or a packet of dried beans or peas, for 'blind' baking

a 20cm (8in) flan tin, about 3½cm (1½in) deep

Be very careful when you remove the hot foil and beans.

1. To make the pastry, follow the steps on page 76. Line the tin with the pastry, then 'blind' bake the pastry case. When it is cooked, take it out of the oven.

The hot baking sheet helps the bottom of the tart to cook.

2. Put the hot baking tray back into the oven on its own. Reduce the temperature of the oven to 170°C, 325°F, gas mark 3. Then, prepare the filling for the tart.

3. Put the butter and sugar into a large bowl and beat them together until they are light and fluffy. Add a tablespoon of ground almonds and beat it in.

4. Break the egg into a small bowl and beat it well with a fork. Add the egg to the mixture in the large bowl, a little at a time, beating it well after each addition.

Chef's Tip

You could use tinned pears instead of fresh pears. Arrange them on top of the frangipane. Or, try making the tart with other fruits too.

5. Add the remaining ground almonds and beat them into the mixture. Sift in the flour. Then, gently stir the mixture until all the ingredients are mixed together.

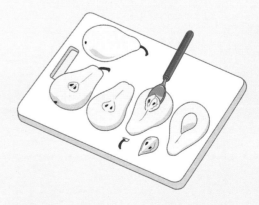

6. Put a pear onto a chopping board. Cut it in half lengthways, from the stalk to the base. Using a small teaspoon, scoop out the core in the middle of each half.

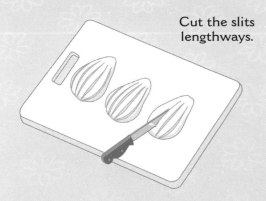

Cut the slits lengthways.

Arrange the pears like this.

7. Using a sharp knife, carefully peel the pears. Put each piece flat side down on the chopping board. Cut five slits two-thirds of the way into the thick end of each piece.

8. Spoon the frangipane into the pastry case. Spread it out using the back of the spoon. Arrange the pears on top, flat side down, with the thin ends in the middle.

9. Bake the tart in the oven for 30-35 minutes, until the pastry case and filling are dark golden. Carefully take the tart out of the oven. Put it on a wire rack to cool.

10. For the glaze, mix the apricot jam and lemon juice together in a small bowl. Brush the glaze over the top of the warm tart, using a pastry brush.

Strawberry tarts

These little tarts are filled with delicious lemony cream and topped with juicy strawberries. You could make them with other fruits. Try raspberries, kiwi fruits or grapes.

Ingredients:

Makes 12 tarts

For the pastry:
175g (6oz) plain flour
25g (1oz) icing sugar
100g (4oz) chilled butter
1 medium egg
2 teaspoons cold water

For the filling:
300g (10oz) small strawberries
3 tablespoons lemon curd
    (see the recipe on pages 52-53
    to make your own)
100ml (4fl oz) double cream

For the glaze:
4 tablespoons redcurrant jelly

a 7½cm (3in) round cutter
a 12-hole shallow bun tray

Chef's Tip

When the pastry cases are cooked, brush the insides with melted redcurrant jelly, before you fill them. This will help to stop the pastry from going soft.

Take the plastic foodwrap off the pastry.

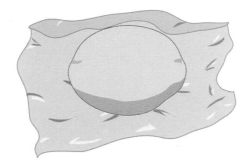

1. Follow the steps on page 76 to make the pastry. Take it out of the fridge and leave it for ten minutes to soften slightly. Heat the oven to 200°C, 400°F, gas mark 6.

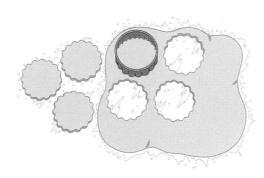

3. Cut circles from the pastry with the cutter. Squeeze the scraps into a ball and roll them out again, then cut more circles. Put a pastry circle in each hole in the bun tray.

Put the strawberries on a chopping board to cut them.

5. Put the strawberries in a colander and rinse them under cold water. Put them on some kitchen paper to dry. Carefully, cut off the green stalks with a sharp knife.

Sprinkle flour onto the rolling pin.

2. Put the pastry on a floury surface. Roll over the pastry once, then turn it. Carry on rolling out the pastry until it is about 30cm (12in) across and 3mm (¼in) thick.

4. Use a fork to prick each pastry case several times. Bake them for 10-12 minutes until they are golden brown. Take them out of the oven and leave them in the tin to cool.

6. Spoon the lemon curd into a bowl. Add one tablespoon of cream and stir it in. Pour the rest of the cream into another bowl. Using a whisk, whisk it until it is just thick.

Use a teaspoon to spoon the filling into each pastry case.

7. Add the lemony mixture to the whipped cream and stir it in. Use your fingers to lift the pastry cases onto a wire rack. Spoon two teaspoons of filling into each case.

Make sure the cut sides face down.

8. Place one whole strawberry in the middle of each tart. Cut the rest of the strawberries in half and arrange them around the whole strawberry.

Let the glaze cool a little before you brush it over the tarts.

9. Put the redcurrant jelly in a pan with two teaspoons of water. Gently heat the pan until the jelly has melted. Using a pastry brush, brush the glaze over the tarts.

Chocolate and raspberry tart

This chocolate tart is made with an orange flavoured pastry, a rich, mousse-like filling and fresh raspberries. You could decorate it with orange rind, icing sugar and mint leaves.

Ingredients:

Serves 8

For the pastry:
1 medium orange
175g (6oz) plain flour
25g (1oz) icing sugar
100g (4oz) butter
1 egg

For the filling:
175g (6oz) plain chocolate drops
2 medium eggs
175ml (6fl oz) double cream
75g (3oz) soft light brown sugar
1 tablespoon orange juice

To decorate:
175g (6oz) fresh raspberries
orange rind
1 tablespoon icing sugar
fresh mint

baking beans, or a packet of
 dried beans or peas

a 20cm (8in) flan tin, about
 3½cm (1½in) deep

Chef's Tip

When you take the tart out of the oven, the filling should be just set and slightly soft in the middle. The filling will get firmer as the tart cools.

1. Grate the rind of the orange on the small holes of a grater. Cut the orange in half and squeeze out the juice. Stir together the rind and two teaspoons of juice in a bowl.

Save the rest of the orange juice to use in the filling.

2. Follow steps 1-3 on page 76 to start making the pastry. At step 4 on page 76, add the rind and orange juice to the yolk, instead of adding water.

3. Finish making the pastry dough, following steps 5-7 on page 76. Then, follow all the steps on page 77 to line the pastry case and bake it 'blind'.

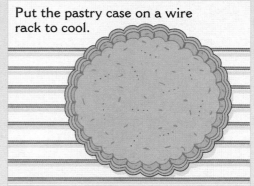

Put the pastry case on a wire rack to cool.

4. Take the cooked pastry out of the oven. Put the hot baking tray back into the oven on its own. Reduce the temperature of the oven to 160°C, 325°F, gas mark 3.

5. For the filling, put the chocolate drops into a heatproof bowl. Pour about 5cm (2in) of water into a pan. Heat it until the water bubbles. Remove it from the heat.

6. Wearing oven gloves, carefully put the bowl inside the pan. Stir the chocolate until it melts. Then, lift the bowl out of the pan. Let the chocolate cool for ten minutes.

7. Break the eggs into a large bowl and beat them with a fork. Add the cream, sugar and one tablespoon of orange juice. Mix them together with a wooden spoon.

8. Pour the melted chocolate into the large bowl, a little at a time, stirring it well between each addition. Then, pour the mixture into the pastry case.

9. Bake the tart for 30 minutes, until the filling is firm. Take it out of the oven. When it is cool, decorate it with raspberries, orange rind, sifted icing sugar and fresh mint.

Crispy apple pies

These crispy pies are
made with apples and
cranberries, flavoured with
orange and cinnamon.

Ingredients:

Makes 12 pies

100g (4oz) filo pastry
1 medium orange
4 eating apples
50g (2oz) dried cranberries
50g (2oz) caster sugar
½ teaspoon cinnamon
50g (2oz) butter
2 teaspoons icing sugar
a 12-hole muffin or deep
   bun tray

1. Heat the oven to 190°C, 375°F, gas mark 5. Take the filo pastry out of the fridge, but leave it in its wrappings. Use the small holes of a grater to grate the orange rind.

2. Cut the orange in half and squeeze out the juice. Cut the apple into quarters. Peel them, then cut out the cores. Cut the quarters into small chunks.

Put the lid back on in between stirring.

3. Put the apple, orange rind and three tablespoons of orange juice into a pan. Heat it gently for 20 minutes, stirring often. Stir in the cranberries, sugar and cinnamon.

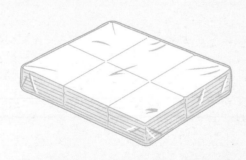

4. Cook the mixture for another five minutes. Take the pan off the heat. Unwrap the pastry and cut each sheet into six squares. Cover it with plastic foodwrap.

5. Put the butter into a small saucepan and melt it gently over a low heat. Use a pastry brush to brush a little butter over one of the pastry squares.

Press the pastry gently into the hole.

6. Put the square into a hole in the tray, buttered side up. Brush butter onto another square. Put it over the first one, so the corners overlap. Butter and add a third square.

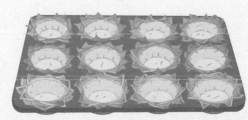

7. Repeat in all the holes. Bake the pastry cases in the oven for ten minutes. Leave them in the tray for five minutes to cool. Then, take the cases out of the tray.

8. Heat the apples again for two minutes until they bubble. Spoon the mixture into the cases, so they are almost full. Then, sift a little icing sugar over the pies.

Plum tarts

Top these golden puff
pastry tarts with
juicy red plums, tossed
together with sugar
and spice.

Ingredients:

Makes 14 tarts

375g (13oz) packet of
   ready-rolled puff pastry
300g (12oz) red plums
1 thick slice white bread
50g (2oz) butter
50g (2oz) soft light brown sugar
½ teaspoon ground mixed spice
4 tablespoons apricot jam

6½cm (2½in) round cutter

1. Heat the oven to 220°C, 425°F,
gas mark 7. Take the pastry out of
the fridge and leave it out for
15-20 minutes. Carefully, cut the
plums in half with a sharp knife.

2. Remove the stones from the
plums. Put them on a chopping
board, cut side down. Cut each
one into small chunks. Put the
chunks into a large mixing bowl.

Chef's Tip

In the next step, you'll be making breadcrumbs. You can make them in a food processor, or grate some bread on the big holes of a grater. Slightly stale bread works best.

3. Make the slices of bread into breadcrumbs. Gently heat the butter in a small frying pan until it has just melted. Pour half of the melted butter into a small bowl.

4. Turn up the heat a little. Add the breadcrumbs to the butter in the frying pan. Fry them for about five minutes, stirring them often, until they are brown and crisp.

5. Remove the pan from the heat. When the breadcrumbs have cooled, add them to the plums, with the sugar and spice. Use your hands to toss everything together.

6. Unroll the pastry. Use the cutter to cut out 14 circles. Put the circles on the baking trays, leaving spaces between them. Prick the middle of each square twice with a fork.

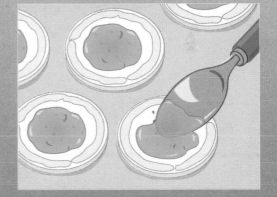

7. Brush some butter from the bowl around the edge of each circle. Make a border about 1cm (½in) wide. Spoon half a teaspoon of jam into the middle of each one.

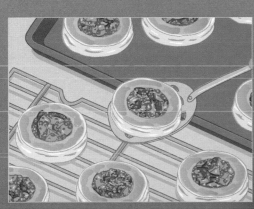

8. Spoon some plums onto the jam. Bake the tarts for 12-15 minutes. When the edges are brown and risen, take them out of the oven. Lift them onto a wire rack to cool.

Chocolate choux buns

These light and airy pastry buns are filled with a vanilla cream and have a lovely smooth chocolate topping.

Ingredients:

Makes 15 buns

For the pastry:
65g (2½oz) plain flour
2 medium eggs
50g (2oz) butter
150ml (¼ pint) water

For the vanilla cream:
200ml (7fl oz) whipping cream
½ teaspoon vanilla essence
1 tablespoon icing sugar
For different flavours of cream,
   see page 74.

For the chocolate topping:
100g (4oz) plain chocolate drops
25g (1oz) butter, softened
2 tablespoons water

Shake off the water.

1. Heat the oven to 220°C, 425°F, gas mark 7. Using a paper towel, wipe some butter over two baking trays. Hold each baking tray under the cold tap for a few seconds.

2. Sift the flour through a sieve onto a piece of baking parchment and put it to one side. Then, break the eggs into a small bowl and beat them with a fork.

3. Cut the butter into small pieces and put it into a saucepan with the water. Heat the pan very gently over a low heat. As soon as the mixture boils, take it off the heat.

4. Straight away, tip all the flour into the pan. Stir it in for about a minute, until the mixture begins to form a ball in the middle of the pan. Let it cool for five minutes.

5. Add a little egg. Stir it in well, then repeat this until you've added all the egg. Then, put teaspoonfuls of pastry onto the baking trays, leaving spaces between them.

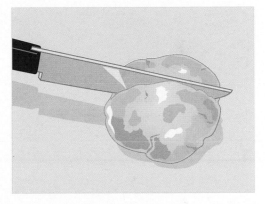

6. Bake the buns for 10 minutes, then turn down the heat to 190°C, 375°F, gas mark 5. Bake the buns for another 25 minutes until they are puffy and dark golden.

7. Lift the baking trays out of the oven and put the buns onto a wire rack, using a spatula. Then, prick a hole in the side of each one with a sharp knife to let out any steam.

8. While the buns are cooling, make the vanilla cream (see the recipe on page 74). When the buns are completely cold, cut each one in half.

9. Fill the buns with the vanilla cream. For the topping, pour 5cm (2in) of water into a pan. Heat it until the water bubbles, then remove it from the heat.

10. Put the chocolate drops into a heatproof bowl, with the butter and two tablespoons of water. Put the bowl into the pan. Stir the ingredients until they are smooth.

11. Lift the bowl out of the pan. Using a teaspoon, carefully coat the top of each bun with some chocolate topping. Leave the buns on the wire rack to set.

Fruit scones

These fruit scones are delicious filled with jam and whipped cream. You could also fill them with home-made lemon curd (see pages 52-53 for the recipe).

Ingredients:

Makes 9 scones

200g (8oz) self-raising flour
50g (2oz) caster sugar
50g (2oz) margarine
¼ teaspoon salt
100g (4oz) sultanas
1 medium egg
75ml (5 tablespoons) milk

strawberry jam and whipped
  cream for the filling

6cm or 7cm (2½in) round cutter

1. Heat the oven to 220°C, 425°F, gas mark 7. Grease a baking tray with cooking oil. Sift the flour into a large bowl. Add the sugar, margarine and salt.

Chef's Tip

In the next step, you will add the sultanas. You could use the same amount of chopped glacé cherries or dates, if you prefer – or you could leave them out altogether.

2. Use your fingertips to rub the margarine into the sugar and flour. When the mixture looks like fine breadcrumbs, stir in the sultanas with a wooden spoon.

3. Break the egg into a small bowl and beat it well with a fork. Add the milk to the egg and stir it in. Put one tablespoon of the eggy mixture into a cup to use later.

4. Pour the eggy mixture from the small bowl into the large bowl, a little at a time. Stir the mixture well between each addition. The mixture should form a soft dough.

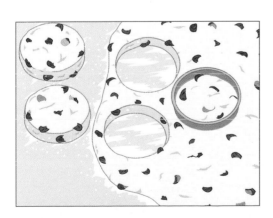

5. Sprinkle your work surface with flour and put the dough onto it. Lightly roll out the dough until it is about 1½cm (½in) thick. Use the cutter to cut out circles.

Leave a space between each scone.

6. Squeeze the scraps of dough into a ball. Roll them out again. Cut out more circles. Put all the circles on the tray. Brush the tops with the eggy mixture from the cup.

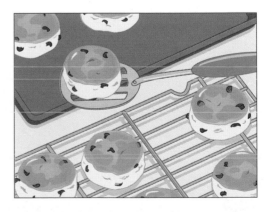

7. Bake the scones in the oven for ten minutes until they are golden. Carefully take them out of the oven. Use a spatula to lift them onto a wire rack to cool.

Cinnamon bread rolls

These delicious bread rolls are flavoured with cinnamon and raisins. Bread is made with yeast and special flour called 'strong flour' or 'bread flour'. The yeast makes the dough rise, so the bread is light to eat. To make it rise, you'll need to leave the dough in a warm place for over an hour. You'll need plenty of time to make this recipe.

Ingredients:

Makes 16 rolls

450g (1lb) strong white
   bread flour
2 teaspoons caster sugar
1½ teaspoons salt
2 teaspoons cinnamon
1½ teaspoons dried
   easy-blend yeast
75g (3oz) raisins
275ml (9fl oz) milk
25g (1oz) butter
1 egg

1. Sift the flour into a large bowl. Stir in the sugar, salt, cinnamon, yeast and raisins. Make a hollow in the middle.

The mixture should be lukewarm, not hot.

2. Put the milk and butter into a pan and heat it very gently until the butter has just melted. Take the pan off the heat.

3. Pour the milky mixture into the hollow in the flour. Stir it in well until it no longer sticks to the sides of the bowl.

Sprinkle the work surface with flour.

4. To knead the dough, press the heels of both hands, or your knuckles, into the dough. Push it away from you firmly.

5. Fold the dough in half and turn it around. Push the dough away from you again. Then, fold it in half and turn it around again.

6. Carry on pushing the dough away from you, folding it and turning it for ten minutes, until it feels smooth and springy.

7. Dip a paper towel in cooking oil and rub it inside a bowl. Put the dough in the bowl and cover it with foodwrap.

8. Leave the dough in a warm place for about 45 minutes, until the dough has risen to twice its original size.

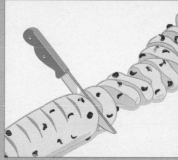

9. Knead the dough again, for a minute, to squeeze out any air bubbles. Then, cut the dough into 16 pieces.

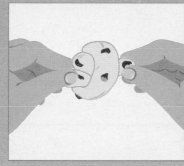

10. Roll each piece of dough to make a 'sausage' about 20cm (8in) long. Tie each one into a knot.

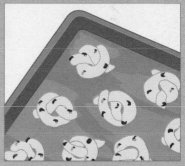

11. Grease a baking tray with cooking oil and put the rolls onto it. Heat your oven to 220°C, 425°F, gas mark 7.

12. Rub some plastic foodwrap with oil, then cover the rolls. Put them back in a warm place for 20 minutes to rise again.

13. Beat the egg in a small bowl. Take the foodwrap off the rolls. Brush each roll with some of the beaten egg.

The rolls will become golden brown.

14. Bake the rolls for 10-12 minutes. Leave them on the tray for a few minutes, then put them on a wire rack to cool.

Chef's Tip

To tell if your bread rolls have cooked, carefully turn one over and tap it with your finger. It should sound hollow.

Baking skills

There are many simple skills which cooks use when they are baking, but they're not all obvious when you start. These pages show you some hints and tips that will help you when you're baking.

Breaking an egg

1. Crack the egg sharply on the edge of a cup or bowl. Push your thumbs into the crack and pull the shell apart.

2. Slide the egg into the cup or bowl. Pick out any pieces of shell, before you add the egg to a mixture.

Separating eggs

Break an egg onto a plate. Cover the yolk with an egg cup. Hold the egg cup, while you tip the plate so the egg white slides off.

Beating eggs

To beat eggs, break them into a bowl. Then, use a fork to stir them quickly, mixing the yolks and whites together.

Whisking egg whites

Put the bowl on a damp cloth to stop it from slipping.

1. Pour the egg whites into a clean, dry bowl, making sure no yolk gets in. Hold the bowl tightly in one hand.

2. Using your other hand, twist the whisk around and around quickly in the bowl. The egg will begin to go white and frothy.

3. Carry on whisking the egg whites until stiff points or 'peaks' form on the top, when you lift the whisk, like this.

Sifting

You need to sift some ingredients, such as flour, to get rid of lumps. Put the flour in a sieve over a bowl. Shake the sieve.

Beating a mixture

Stir the mixture briskly with a wooden spoon. Carry on until the mixture is smooth and has no lumps in it.

Folding in

To fold ingredients together, slice into them with a metal spoon and gently turn them over until they are evenly mixed.

Rubbing in

1. Cut the butter into pieces. Using a wooden spoon, coat it with flour. Use your fingertips to rub the butter into the flour.

2. Lift the mixture and let it fall back into the bowl as you rub. Carry on until the mixture looks like breadcrumbs.

Chocolate drops melt quickly, but you can use pieces of chocolate instead.

Rolling out

Dust the rolling pin with flour.

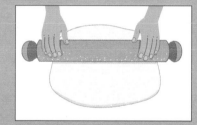

1. Dust a clean, dry work surface with flour. Put the dough onto it. Press the rolling pin onto the dough and roll it away from you.

2. Turn the dough a little and roll it again. Carry on rolling and turning the dough until it is the thickness you need.

Melting chocolate

Stir with a wooden spoon.

1. Put the chocolate into a heatproof bowl. Heat about 5cm (2in) of water in a pan until it is bubbling gently.

2. Remove the pan from the heat. Then, wearing oven gloves, lift the bowl into the pan. Stir the chocolate as it melts.

Testing cakes

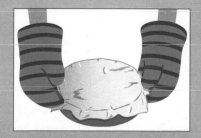

At the end of the cooking time, test the cake to see if it is cooked. Press it in the middle. If it is cooked, it will feel firm and springy.

In some recipes, you will need to cover the cake with foil to stop it from burning. Put it back in the oven to finish cooking.

Turning out cakes

1. Run a knife around the sides of the tin to loosen the cake. Hold a plate, slightly larger than the tin, over the tin.

2. Turn the tin and plate over together, so the cake turns out onto the plate. Then, carefully lift the tin off the cake.

Index

Edited by Jane Chisholm; Art director: Mary Cartwright; Digital imaging: Nick Wakeford and John Russell.
With thanks to Non Figg, Jo Thompson, Katrina Fearn, Abigail Wheatley, Brian Voakes and Erica Harrison.